# Lakeside and Haverthwaite Railway

by

H. I. Quayle, M.A., A.M.B.I.M.

and S. C. Jenkins, M.A.

DALESMAN BOOKS
1977

The Dalesman Publishing Company Ltd.,
Clapham (via Lancaster), North Yorkshire.

First published 1977



ISBN: 0 85206 409 8

Printed in Great Britain by
Galava Printing Co. Ltd., Hallam Road, Nelson, Lancashire.

# Contents



The cover photographs show:— Front: 2-6-4T No. 2085 heading a Haverthwaite—Lakeside train near Newby Bridge in May 1975 (W. H. Ashcroft). Back:— Top: 2MT No. 46441 arriving at Lakeside on the "Lake Windermere Cruise" train on June 24th, 1964 (British Railways). Bottom: 2-6-4T No. 2085 piloting 0-6-0ST "Cumbria" out of Haverthwaite with an enthusiasts' special (Lakeside Railway Society).

Photographs in the text are on pages 33-36 and 53-56.

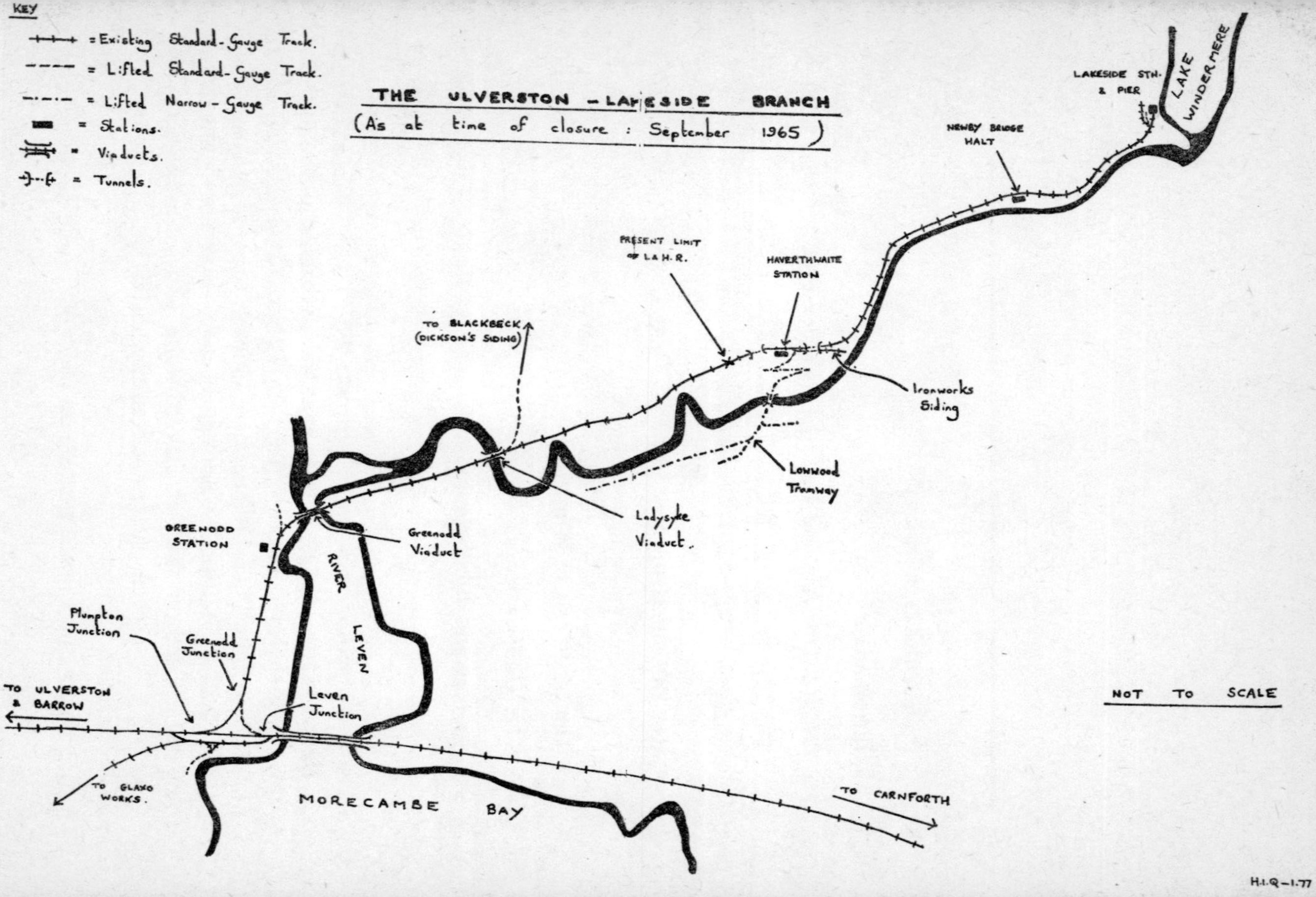

KEY
= Existing Standard-Gauge Track.
= Lifted Standard-Gauge Track.
= Lifted Narrow-Gauge Track.
= Stations.
= Viaducts.
= Tunnels.
THE ULVERSTON - LAKESIDE BRANCH
(As at time of closure : September 1965)
LAKESIDE STN. & PIER
LAKE WINDERMERE
NEWBY BRIDGE HALT
PRESENT LIMIT OF L&H.R.
HAVERTHWAITE STATION
TO BLACKBECK (DICKSON'S SIDING)
Ironworks Siding
Lowwood Tramway
Ladyside Viaduct.
Greenodd Viaduct
GREENODD STATION
RIVER
LEVEN
Plumpton Junction
Greenodd Junction
Leven Junction
TO ULVERSTON & BARROW
TO GLAXO WORKS.
MORECAMBE BAY
TO CARNFORTH
NOT TO SCALE
H.I.Q-1.77

# Preface

## by O. S. Nock

THE Furness Railway branch from Ulverston to Lakeside was one of the first North Country lines that I came to know well, after my father's business was moved from Reading to Barrow-in-Furness in 1916. At that stage in the first world war one could still make attractive and very cheap day excursions into the Lake District, and the run from Ulverston to Lakeside was my first introduction to that marvellous region I came to love so well. In later years I knew the country surrounding the line as well as the railway itself, because Newby Bridge was a cycle run from where we lived, near Furness Abbey, that I could do comfortably out and home, between breakfast and lunch time or between lunch and tea.

So I welcome this delightful little book that the authors have written in such careful and affectionate detail. I am especially interested in the early history, long before I knew the line personally, and for the memories of my boyhood that the later chapters have aroused.

**February 1977** **O. S. Nock**

# Introduction

THE Lakeside & Haverthwaite Railway originated in the 1860s as a branch of the old Furness Railway. Always associated with the varied industries of the Leven Valley, the line was and still is an important tourist amenity in southern Lakeland. This small volume—which is the first history of the Lakeside line ever published—traces the history of the branch from its origins to the present day. The story of the line is complemented by chapters devoted to the railway steamers on Windermere, and to the local gunpowder industry which gave rise to two interesting minor railways.

The authors have had much first-hand knowledge of the line. H. I. Quayle, who is now a business analyst with a well known industrial fertiliser manufacturer, was publicity officer of the Lakeside Railway Society from 1970 to 1973, and has concentrated mainly on the preservation era, together with the gunpowder tramways. S. C. Jenkins, a founder member of the University of Lancaster Transport & Industrial Archaeological Society (affiliated to the L.R.S.), has concentrated on the historical side of the narrative, and has also contributed the chapter on the steamers.

**Oxford, 1977**

**Acknowledgements**

The authors would like to thank the multitude of people without whose help, advice and encouragement this book would never have been written. We are grateful to Mr. O. S. Nock for kindly consenting to write the foreword, to Mr. Tom Clark of Barrow for supplying so much valuable background information and to the various members of the Lakeside Railway Society who have contributed material.

# 1. Origins, Opening and Early Years(1869-1900)

THE Lakeside & Haverthwaite Railway was born in the late 1860s, as a result of the Furness Railway's drive to develop the southern Lake District as a popular tourist area. The Furness had itself originated some two decades earlier, primarily to provide transport for the rich deposits of iron ore that were to be found in the Furness region, but by the 1860s the company's directors were well aware of the tourist potential of the area through which their railway ran.

**The Genesis of the Lake District Tourist Industry**

The popularity of the Lake District was a concomitant of the "Romantic" movement in art and literature, which began to make itself felt in the late 18th century. The Cumberland, Westmorland and Furness district had traditionally been regarded as remote, inhospitable and savage by the classically-educated English aristocracy; and much of the area—especially the high fell regions—was just as they imagined it to be. Celia Fiennes, the intrepid seventeenth-century traveller and topographer, found "villages of sad little huts made up of dry walls", in the highlands north of "Winander Water". They had, she recorded, "... no mortar or plaster within or without; for the most part I took them at first sight for a sort of house or barns to fodder cattle in, not thinking them to be dwelling houses". (1) The idea of spending a holiday in such a wilderness was unthinkable to the cultivated 18th century mind; the typical 18th century holidaymaker preferred to spend his ample leisuretime travelling abroad—ideally amid the classical ruins of Italy or Greece. The Romantic movement, however, changed all this; where classical thinking had demanded harmony of shape and form, and applauded "reason", the romantics gloried in the wild and the picturesque. It became fashionable to journey to the hitherto neglected districts of the British Isles — to Wales, the West Country and the Scottish Highlands, and the upper class "holidaymakers" of late 18th century England began to journey along the rough, unmade roads to the wilds in ever-increasing numbers.

The great war waged against Revolutionary and Napoleonic France at the end of the 18th and the beginning of the 19th centuries meant that Englishmen could no longer travel abroad, and this further boosted the popularity of the new English "tourist regions". Turnpike roads enabled the journey west to the mountains to be undertaken in greater comfort and safety, and by the end of the wars (1815) many residents of towns such as Kendal and Lancaster looked forward to visits and holidays in such small resorts as Rampside, Grange-over-Sands and Silverdale. (2) The Lake District, then, was opened up to the public—or at least the upper and upper-middle classes—by roads. It was the coming of the railways, however, that caused the great Victorian "take-off" in the holiday industry; the romantics, led by such well known publicists as William Wordsworth, Harriet Martineau and John Ruskin, created a demand—which the railways were not slow in fulfilling.

**The Coming of the Railways**

The first railway to influence the Lake District was the Lancaster and Preston Junction, which opened in 1840 and was soon conveying travellers to the south-east corner of the region, from whence coaches carried the early holidaymakers on into the fells. The Lancaster & Carlisle, opened some six years later as part of a through route to Scotland, also linked the Lancaster & Preston Junction to the Maryport & Carlisle, while the Furness Railway—which reached east to Ulverston by 1854—and the Ulverston & Lancaster (1857) completed a great chain of railways which encircled the entire Lake District. Most of these lines were promoted with a profitable coal and ore traffic in mind, but once built they encouraged tourism in the areas they served. Grange and Arnside, for example, soon developed into select little resorts—indeed, at Grange, the F.R. and its associate, the Grange Hotel Company, created a complete little town with ornamental gardens, station, promenade and hotel—all attractively grouped on the sea-front and executed in a similar architectural style. (3)

Meanwhile, the Victorian developers had reached Windermere. In 1847, the Kendal & Windermere Railway had opened a branch from the Lancaster & Carlisle line to the remote hamlet of Birthwaite—which subsequently mushroomed into the present town of "Windermere". (4) The lake itself became an exceedingly popular tourist attraction; by 1850 there were four steamers in operation, and mid-Victorian tourists were able to savour the scenic delights of the 12-mile voyage between Waterhead at the extreme northern end of the lake and Newby Bridge, the landing place on the river Leven that served as the southern terminus of the steamer service.

The idea of a railway extension to Newby Bridge was first suggested at a meeting of the Furness Railway's board of directors in 1847, but these vague plans did not take concrete form until the 1860s. By this time the company was in a much stronger position—the Ulverston & Lancaster Railway, which was worked by the F.R. from its opening, passed into direct Furness ownership in 1862, and so gave the company a secure strategic position in the southern coastal areas of the Lake District. (5) Moreover, the Windermere tourist business had gone from strength to strength; the two rival steamship operators—the Windermere Steam Yacht Company and the Windermere Iron Steamboat Company—had amalgamated to form the Windermere United Steam Yacht Company (6), and were contemplating the purchase of a new steamer. Clearly, a railway connecting these popular steamer services to the growing Furness system would be a profitable investment, even though the holiday traffic tended to be of a seasonal nature. Not only would such a railway earn revenue from the large numbers of holidaymakers and excursionists that would be carried—it would also enable the railway company to secure a controlling interest in the lucrative steamers themselves. The company therefore decided to construct a branch from their main line at Plumpton, near Ulverston, to a terminus at Newby Bridge, via the natural routeway formed by the valley of the river Leven which flows down from Windermere to the sea near Ulverston.

The route would follow the broad estuary of the river as far as the small shipping village of Greenodd, and then head towards the industrial settlement of Backbarrow before striking up into the hills towards the lake. The upper part of the line would be a difficult one to engineer, with several rock cuttings and two tunnels, but against this the completed railway would include fine estuarial and mountain scenery and at the same time profit from the traffic generated by the area's numerous local industries. These included important gunpowder mills at Black Beck and Low Wood, a cotton mill and ironworks at Backbarrow (all of which were near Haverthwaite) and a small bobbin mill near Newby Bridge.

The company had obtained Parliamentary sanction for a two-mile branch to Greenodd before making a definite decision on the Windermere line, and as this earlier scheme utilised the first part of the projected Leven Valley route it was only necessary to obtain powers for the upper part of the branch. A Bill for a railway from Greenodd to Newby Bridge was therefore prepared, and it was sent up to Parliament in October 1865. The Bill received the royal assent in the following year, and James Ramsden—the general manager of the Furness Railway and a leader of the Furness industrial elite—cut the first sod at Haverthwaite on November 22nd, 1866. (7) Construction began in earnest in the following year under the overall supervision of Messrs. McClean & Stileman of London, but with Colonel Strongitharm—a well known local personality—acting as resident engineer. The main contract for the works went to Messrs. Benton & Woodiwiss, and Mr. William Gradwell of Barrow secured the station contracts. (8)

The line wrought great changes in the valley area. The embankments needed to carry the railway along the side of the estuary enabled a considerable portion of land to be reclaimed along the Plumpton to Greenodd section, while at Haverthwaite the line approached the village on a large embankment and then plunged through a 165-yard tunnel. The station itself was to be sited on a narrow shelf of land to the north of the Greenodd to Levens Bridge turnpike, and an extensive cutting was necessary in order to make room for the rather cramped platforms and sidings. A second tunnel, some 87 yards in length, enabled the line to escape from the confines of Haverthwaite station yard and strike north along the wooded valley of the Leven. Two substantially-built bridges were necessary in the Greenodd area, one across the channel formed by the confluence of the rivers Leven and Crake, and the other across the Leven at Lady Syke—about ¾-mile from Greenodd station. The line was not, then, a particularly easy one to build, and the work soon fell behind schedule.

Meanwhile, the directors had decided to extend the line on to a new terminus at Lakeside, about a mile beyond Newby Bridge. This would allow the Windermere steamers to come alongside the trains at a deep water quay at the southern end of the lake, rather than risk the slightly risky voyage down the shallow waters of the Leven to Newby Bridge—a wise and far-sighted move that enabled bigger and better steamers to be introduced in later years. The 7 mile 73 chain branch was finally ready for its Board of Trade inspection in April, 1869, and, although the stations were not yet completed, the line was passed for opening on Saturday, April 28th, and ceremonially opened on Tuesday, June 1st.

**The Railway Opens**

The official "first train" to run on the Lakeside branch left Barrow at 07-30, behind locomotive No. 21—one of the well-known Sharp Stewart 2-2-2 well tanks used by the Furness Railway on its local services. In brilliant, springtime weather, the colourful "Indian red" engine and its train of 4-wheeled coaches set off down the Furness main line and reached Ulverston—the "junction" for the Lakeside line—at about 08-00. The reporter from the "Barrow Herald" recorded that the engine was "gaily and beautifully decorated with evergreens, flowers, banners bearing the national insignia, Union Jacks, and from the centre of the engine rose an arch wreathed with flowers and evergreens and surmounted by the Prince of Wales's feathers".

Several people boarded the train at Ulverston, and it then proceeded along the main line to the newly-formed junction at Plumpton. The train then diverged onto the recently constructed branch line, and commenced its historic journey to Lakeside. At Greenodd a large crowd cheered as the train entered the unfinished station, and more passengers entrained from the temporary wooden platform. Crossing the iron girder bridge at the northern end of Greenodd station, the first-day special continued on its way up the branch. At Haverthwaite, yet more crowds and flags welcomed the train as it laboured its way up through the tunnels, while still more waited at the temporary wooden station at Lakeside. The customary speeches and tributes were made, and the officials, dignitaries and other important first-day travellers then retired for refreshments. Although the railway was now officially open, much work lay ahead before it was finished: indeed, the people of Haverthwaite, Low Wood and Backbarrow began to think that the railway did not intend to provide them with a passenger station at all! Eventually, however, the new station buildings at Greenodd, Haverthwaite and Lakeside started to take shape.

The two through stations at Greenodd and Haverthwaite were built to a standard Furness Railway design, which provided accommodation for the stationmasters and their families, together with the usual booking offices and waiting rooms. These distinctive buildings were about 90 feet long, and 18 feet wide, and faced low platforms. They were constructed of "patent white bricks", which were supplied by a Leeds firm, and had local Lake District slates on their roofs. The use of the decorative (and expensive) Flemish Bonding, offset by horizontal bands of vitrified purple-black stretchers, showed that the Furness was prepared to build in style on its new tourist line. This love of visual display was even more apparent at Lakeside, and caused one or two shareholders to complain about the cost of the opulent new structures. Officially described as an example of "the Italian style of architecture", and later described by Mr. O. S. Nock as "a miniature edition of Fishguard Harbour or Harwich (Parkeston Quay)", the Lakeside terminus was a combined railway station and steamer pier. Two platforms — one 745 ft. and the other 205 ft long—were constructed parallel to a 633 ft. pier, and covered with a 206 ft. train shed. An extensive range of buildings at the northern end of the train shed and at 90 degrees to the lake, housed the main offices and other facilities, while a long veranda ran parallel to the lake and the platforms. The whole structure was two storeys high, and like Greenodd and Haverthwaite stations it was built of white bricks with black bands, together with red brick and red sandstone quoins. A "Palm

# PLATFORM ELEVATION & PLAN OF HAVERTHWAITE STATION BUILDING

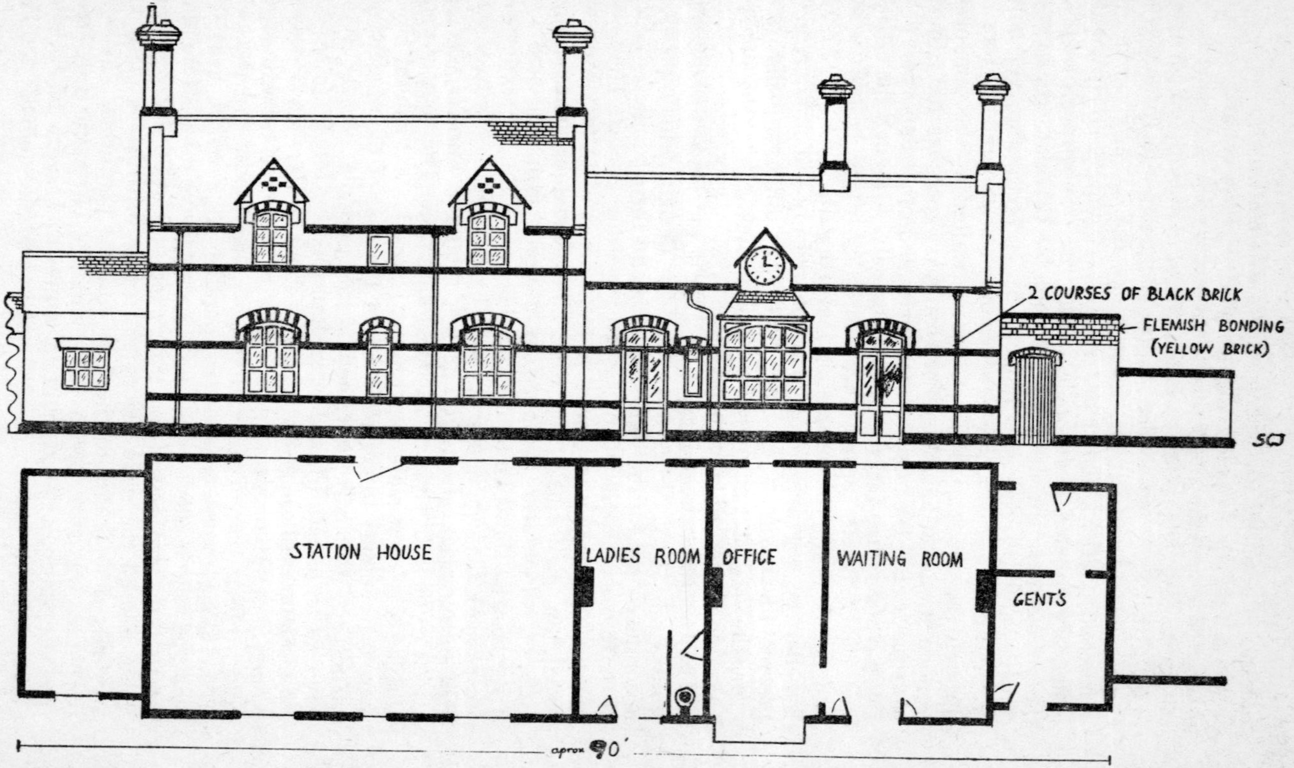

Court" type restaurant and refreshment room was built on top of the veranda, so that well-off Victorian tourists could watch the comings and goings of the steamers while they dined. "From the present aspect of the works", wrote the "Barrow Herald" reporter in 1869, "the station will have a really beautiful appearance when complete". The facilities at Lakeside also included a goods shed, a decorative water tower, lavish signalling and a 42 ft. turntable installed by Messrs. Westray & Foster of Barrow.

Greenodd and Haverthwaite stations were provided with goods sheds, signal boxes and standard Furness pattern signal boxes in addition to the main station buildings. All of these structures were built in what could, with some justification, be called, the "Lakeside Branch" style of architecture; every building on the line was constructed of the ubiquitous white bricks with contrasting trimmings—a feature which did much to give the line a distinct character of its own, even though it was a part of a much larger concern. A fourth station—Newby Bridge—was only a small halt, with a tiny shelter on a single platform; no sidings or other facilities were ever provided.

The branch was double as far as Greenodd and single thereafter, with an intermediate passing loop provided at Haverthwaite. At Plumpton, an east-to-north curve was laid to enable through trains to run direct to Lakeside without reversing at Ulverston. This curve—which ran from a junction on the main line, known as Leven Junction, to "Greenodd Junction" on the branch—was laid mainly for the benefit of the Midland Railway, and underlines the close links then being fostered between Derby and Barrow; indeed, there had even been talk of an amalgamation, and it has been suggested that the lavish station accommodation provided at Lakeside is evidence of the Midland's interest in the scheme.

**Early Days**

The new railway prospered, with a diverse freight traffic, as well as a modest local passenger business and the summer excursion trains. Inwards freight traffic included coal for the steamers, saltpetre and sulphur for the gunpowder works at Low Wood and Black Beck, ore for the Backbarrow ironworks, and building materials for the numerous desirable residences and hotels that the developers were erecting in the Windermere area. Outwards freight traffic consisted mainly of pig iron from Backbarrow, gunpowder, and pit props—for the area was heavily wooded and had a flourishing coppice industry. In addition to these major sources of freight, the railway carried thousands of hampers of bobbins from the Stott Park Mill, near Lakeside, and cartons of dye from the ultramarine works at Backbarrow (set up in the former cotton mills, which shut down just before the opening of the railway).

Both of the gunpowder mills were provided with rail links; a two mile long standard-gauge branch line connected the Black Beck works with the "main line" at Lady Syke, while at Low Wood an existing 3 ft. 6 ins. narrow gauge system was extended across the Leven and into Haverthwaite goods yard (see chapter 7 for a detailed description of these two interesting private systems). The Backbarrow ironworks also profited from a direct rail connection; an extension of the headshunt at Haverthwaite ran through the east tunnel and ended above the furnaces of the works, enabling ore to be gravity discharged.

The local passenger trains between Lakeside and Ulverston normally consisted of three or four short-wheelbase coaches and a full brake vehicle, headed by one of the Sharp, Stewart 2-2-2 well tanks. Extra coaches were added on Thursdays (Ulverston market day) and Saturdays. Four-wheelers were used until the 1880s, after which six-wheeled vehicles were drafted onto the branch. Journey time was about 25 minutes for the nine mile run. Some trains ran through to Barrow, while numerous specials and excursions were run in connection with local events such as Lakeside Flower Show and Grasmere Sports. It must be emphasised, however, that the numbers of tourists conveyed to Lakeside in the Victorian era remained relatively small—the real boom in the Lake District tourist trade came with the development of holidays with pay in the 20th century.

**Locomotives used on the Branch in the 19th century**

The above mentioned 2-2-2 single-wheelers worked the line for the first twenty years of its existence. There were ten of these locomotives altogether, and all were purchased from Sharp, Stewart & Company between 1852 and 1866. The first four engines had 14 in. by 18 in. inside cylinders and 5 ft. 6 in. driving wheels, but the later batch had 15 in. by 18 in. cylinders. The boiler pressure was 120 lb. per sq. in., and the water capacity was 500 gallons. These quaint little machines were painted in the standard Furness Railway livery of Indian Red, with black and vermilion lining, and sported polished brass domes and safety valve covers. Although it is obviously difficult to say which of the ten 2-2-2WTs were used on the line in the Victorian period, it seems that No. 34—which was one of the later batch—was a regular performer on the Lakeside services, while its sister No. 37 worked the nearby Coniston branch.

These old engines survived until about 1896—the last were disposed of by 1898—and the local passenger services on the line were taken over by a class of seven 2-4-2Ts that had started life as 2-4-0 tender engines back in the 1870s. Originally designed as main line passenger engines, and built by Sharp, Stewart & Co., the conversions were effected by simply extending the frames backwards to take the new bunkers and fitting 1,000 gallon side tanks. The conversions were completed by the addition of radial axles beneath the bunkers. The seven locomotives—out of an original batch of 15 tender engines—were numbered in the following series: 47, 48, and 70 to 74. Of these, Nos. 47 and 72 were regular Lakeside engines.

Goods services were handled by Sharp, Stewart 0-6-0 tender engines—members of a large class of 55 locomotives, delivered at intervals between 1866 and 1884. They were one of Sharp, Stewart's standard designs, and similar machines were delivered to the Cambrian and other railways. Wheels were 4 ft. 6 in. in diameter, and the inside cylinders were 16 in. by 24 in. The original members of the class were cabless, with only a simple weatherboard to protect the crew from the wind and rain. They had smallish boilers surmounted by tall chimneys, domes and elegant brass safety valve covers, but rebuilding altered the external appearance of the class; when the last survivors were withdrawn in 1930 they had all received larger boilers, cabs, and Ramsbottom safety valves, and bore little resemblance to the original design. One of these engines—No. 115—achieved everlasting fame on the morning of November 22nd, 1892; it was waiting at a signal at Lindal (between Ulverston and Barrow) when the driver heard an ominous underground rumbling. Realising what was about to happen, the crew jumped clear before the engine sank slowly into an old mine working. It finally came to rest about 200 feet below ground, and it was decided that a rescue was impossible. The hole was therefore filled in, and the engine has been underground ever since.

These three classes of engine handled most of the trains on the branch in the first 30 years of its life. There were, of course, other types, especially on the summer excursions, but—as was pointed out above—excursion traffic really developed in the early years of the 20th century, and it would therefore be more convenient to mention the sort of motive power used on these trains in the following chapter, which covers the growth of the Furness tourist traffic in greater detail.

(1) *The Journeys of Celia Fiennes* (Everyman edt., p. 196).

(2) Alan Harris "Seaside Resorts of the North West", *Transactions of the Historic Society of Lancashire & Cheshire,* Vol. 115, 1963.

(3) Harris, *loc. cit.*

(4) J. D. Marshall & M. Davies-Shiel, *The Industrial Archaeology of the Lake Counties,* 1969, p. 216.

(5) R. W. Rush, *The Furness Railway,* 1973, pps. 23 sqq.

(6) See below.

(7) *The Barrow Herald,* Saturday, June 5th, 1869.

(8) *Ibid.*

# 2. The Heyday of the Branch (1900-1939)

THE close links between railways, tourism and the growth of the Lake District as a holiday area have already been noted; towns such as Windermere, Grange-over-Sands, Arnside, Morecambe, Blackpool and Southport were the products of a fever of speculation and development sparked off by the coming of the railways. The Lakeside branch was itself the product of the tourist boom, and its construction enabled the Furness Railway to gain control of the popular Windermere steamers. However, as we have seen, the F.R. did little actively to exploit its immense tourist potential during the 19th century; there were, it is true, steamer trips between Fleetwood and Barrow, and these enabled tourists to visit Furness Abbey. There were also one or two railway hotels—notably at Furness Abbey and at Grange—but, generally speaking, the F.R. was not a tourist-orientated line. A series of developments in the last quarter of the 19th century were to change all that.

The Furness depended heavily upon the local iron industry, and when, in the 1870s, that industry went into decline, the railway company suffered accordingly. The long depression—which was a result of competition from imported Spanish ore, a new steel-making process that ended the monopoly of the local haematite ore, and a general slump in trade—hit the F.R. hard; the amount of ore sent from the area fell from 400,000 tons in 1870 to about 10,000 in the mid 1890s, and the company—which had spent vast sums of money on its grandiose Barrow Docks scheme—was forced to effect economies. Services were cut and the timings of the best trains were decelerated. Dividends fell from 10% in the early 1870s to 6½% in 1880, and then down to only 2% in 1886. Things then seemed to improve, and a 5% dividend was paid in 1889. Unfortunately, even if the improvement in general trade continued, the Furness district was still destined to suffer, as the local ore was now starting to run out; when, in 1893, the Midland Railway announced that it intended to abandon Barrow and build a new harbour at Heysham, it seemed that only a miracle could save the unfortunate Furness Railway from financial disaster.

The miracle came. Throughout the 19th century the standard of living of the English working class had improved—imperceptibly at first, and then rapidly as the turn of the century loomed nearer. Several factors caused the improvement, including the momentous reforms of the Victorian era, such as the Factory Acts and the extensions of the franchise, together with increased trade union activity towards the end of the century which tended to raise wage levels. Society became more democratic—both politically and economically—and, for the first time, working men started to look forward to that now solidly-established institution, the annual family holiday. The effect of all this as far as the Lake District is concerned will be obvious. The area was already established as an upper and middle class "playground" and, with the improved standards of living among the workers, they too could afford to visit the Lakes. On top of this, many of them began to stay in the area for one or two weeks—hitherto the small numbers of workers who had visited the Lake District had been day trippers.

The Furness directors seem to have taken some time to realise the true potential of their line as a holiday attraction; probably because the "old order", represented by Ramsden, had fixed ideas about the railway as an ore carrier. In 1895, however, Sir James retired. This 72-year-old man had been a father figure, both to the railway and to the town of Barrow, but he was perhaps too old to see that the company could only survive by adapting itself to new conditions. His successor, on the other hand, immediately grasped the fact that the line had tremendous tourist potential. The new secretary and general manager, Alfred Aslett, had come from the Cambrian Railways—a system very like the Furness in that it was basically a long straggling main line running through remote but beautiful coastal and mountain scenery—and he was therefore admirably fitted to the task of "selling" the Furness to the new generation of holidaymakers.

The Lakeside branch—which connected with the Windermere steamers and was itself a highly scenic line—played an important part in Aslett's new plans. A variety of Lakeland tours were arranged, incorporating travel by rail, steamer and charabanc, and many of these made use of the branch in order to reach the lake. The "Six Lakes Tour" was one of the best of these rail-water-road tours; the excursionists were taken to Lakeside by train, then steamed up to Ambleside by boat. A charabanc carried the tourists on to Ullswater, and they then sailed up to the northern end of this second lake and changed into a charabanc again for the 5½ mile run to Penrith. A journey along the late-lamented Cockermouth, Keswick and Penrith Railway took the intrepid travellers to Keswick, where they once more transferred to road vehicles for the journey back to Ambleside via Derwentwater, Thirlmere, Grasmere and Rydal Water. Finally, a lake and railway trip took the travellers back to their starting points. This ambitious tour cost 13s., and was therefore rather expensive (as well as somewhat tiring!). Other tours were shorter and cheaper; for 6s. 6d. one could travel from Ulverston to Greenodd, and then by road up the Crake Valley to Lakebank, for a cruise up Coniston Lake on the company's small steamer *Gondola.* A charabanc then took the party from Coniston to Ambleside, where they boarded the big Windermere steamers for the trip back to Lakeside and Ulverston.

The great holiday resort of Blackpool—the summer playground of thousands upon thousands of North Western workers—had "taken-off" in the early 1900s; the town had grown from a small fishing village with a population of 1,968 in 1841 to a fashionable seaside town with 8,000 inhabitants by 1871. With the growth of the "holiday habit" among the working classes, the town had developed rapidly, and had a population of 47,000 in 1907. The fact that this teeming, fun-loving hive of likely customers was less than 20 miles from Barrow across Morecambe Bay prompted Aslett to introduce steamer services between Blackpool and the Lake District. The new service enabled yet more permutations to be introduced into the combined tour scheme, and a typical tour conveyed Blackpool trippers to Fleetwood by rail, then across Morecambe Bay to Barrow (or, to be exact, Ramsden Dock station), from where the so-called "Fleetwood Boat Train" departed for the 50 minute ride to Lakeside and a Windermere cruise.

In addition to these ambitious combined tours, numerous excursions were run on the branch in the summer months, and several interesting through workings were introduced—including a through Midland Railway coach from London (St. Pancras). Edwardian railway enthusiasts could sit on the banks of the Leven and watch train after train of packed bogie coaches proceed up the branch, while at Lakeside the graceful steamers would set off from the pier with their decks packed like the stands at a Wembley Cup Final. An orchestra complete with harp and bass viol, was introduced in the Lakeside restaurant, and bands played on the steamers themselves; the Edwardian era was indeed the heyday of the railway and the steamers.

It is to Aslett's credit that he not only identified the need for these popular innovations—he also actively fostered interest in the railway and the Furness district with a vigorous publicity campaign, involving large and attractive posters, handbills and postcards (which cost 3d. for a batch of six and are today collectors' items). A whole range of cheap tickets catered for a diverse assortment of potential travellers, which included golfers, anglers and tennis players, as well as the more usual excursionists and weekenders, and special attention was lavished on station gardens—notably at Grange-over-Sands, where the entire sea-front is an extension of the station! This remarkable campaign succeeded in its efforts to arrest the decline of the railway; Aslett managed to increase passenger traffic by 12% within the first three years of his rule, and when he retired in 1918 passenger receipts had increased by as much as 100%. This did much to make good at least some of the damage caused by the decline of the local iron industry.

The outbreak of war in 1914 meant that the Furness Railway once again became an important artery, carrying vast quantities of heavy freight to and from the iron works in the area, and also to the important naval construction yards and armaments factories at Barrow. Indeed, traffic was so heavy that the L.N.W. and Midland companies (among others) had to lend some of their locomotives and rolling stock to the hard-pressed Furness company. The Lakeside branch played its part in the war effort, carrying workmen into the shipyards at Barrow on specials that started and terminated at Greenodd, and, on a sadder note, by carrying off scores of young men to the front. The long list of names on Haverthwaite war memorial bears mute witness to those who never returned, and one is appalled by the losses sustained in these tiny Lakeland communities.

The hostilities in Europe put an end to the railway's tourist traffic, although train working on the branch was apparently still as smart as ever. O. S. Nock said that in 1916 "conditions were hardly favourable to the faultless working of pure passenger services, but the connections at Ulverston were always smartly made". For example, the 09-15 to Lakeside was scheduled to depart only two minutes after the arrival of the Barrow train, while the 14-18 arrival from Barrow had a connection which left for Lakeside at 14-25. With the cessation of the summer excursions, however, the Leven curve was not needed, and so the rails and sleepers were lifted for use elsewhere. As another wartime economy measure, the attractive blue-and-white Furness coach livery was replaced by a more utilitarian all-over blue. With the end of the Great War in November 1918, things started to return to normal. The conflict had little effect on the popularity of the Lake District as a tourist area. In fact, the horrors of the war in France may even have encouraged people to get away from it all amid the fine scenery of the Lakes and mountains. The steamers were ready for the hordes in the 1919 season, and the Leven Curve was relaid and re-opened in time for the summer excursion traffic in the following year.

Unfortunately, the return of peace saw a return of depression and unemployment in the Furness area; the decline of the iron industry continued, and with the end of the war there was less need for the large army of shipbuilders that had gone to work in the Barrow yards—from a wartime peak of 31,000 in 1917, the labour force fell to 3,150 in 1922. The grouping of railways in 1923 placed the Furness in the hands of the London Midland & Scottish Railway, and the new, larger concern had little need of the extensive F.R. facilities in Barrow, so these too were run-down. Finally, these local troubles were overtaken by the "great depression" of the 1930s. Clearly, the peace that had been won with so much bloodshed was but a hollow victory. On the other hand, the 1920s and 1930s saw a further democratisation of the holiday industry; better pay (among those who could find work) together with new innovations such as motor coaches, motor cars and improved bicycles meant that, in spite of the underlying depression, more and more people could afford to spend their holidays away from home. The period also saw a boom in the economy-type holiday, and the archetypal Lake District holidaymaker emerged as the rucksack-carrying hiker, tramping over the fells and staying in the area's numerous Youth Hostels. These new types of tourists continued to pour into the Lake District by train, and the Lakeside branch, with its associated steamer services, remained busy throughout the 1920s and 1930s. Nevertheless the appearance of motor cars on the roads in ever-increasing numbers boded ill for the future. The writing was clearly on the wall at the end of the 1938 summer timetable when, for the first time, the branch passenger service was withdrawn for the winter. Greenodd, Haverthwaite, and Lakeside stations still accepted parcels traffic each day between 08-00 and 17-00 hours, but, to all intents and purposes, the villagers of the Leven valley had lost their regular passenger service. In 1939 passenger services resumed briefly at Easter before the full summer timetable on May 27th.

The storm-clouds were already gathering over Europe during what was to be the last peaceful summer in England for several years. The short season on the branch was soon over, and the commencement of hostilities almost coincided with the end of the summer timetable.

## The Branch during the War Years

Summer passenger services continued until 1941 and were then suspended for the duration of the war. Freight traffic continued to be heavy, especially to and from the ironworks at Backbarrow. It was, however, the role of Newby Bridge Halt during this period which is of the greatest interest to the railway historian. It has often been stated that special trains carrying prisoners of war were run up the branch as far as the halt, whence they were transferred by road to the camp at Grizedale Hall. However, Grizedale Hall was a camp for German naval and airforce officers, who were never captured in such large numbers as to merit special trains, and the practice seems to have been to move these prisoners, under guard, by normal rail services as far as Ulverston; from there they were taken to Grizedale by Army transport. Nonetheless, there was one special train from Newby Bridge Halt, probably some time in 1941, when about 300 Grizedale-held prisoners of war were taken in great secrecy to a British port for transport to Canada. To avoid going into Ulverston station (and because of the wartime removal of the Leven curve) a halt was made at Plumpton Junction for a change of engines—final destination was presumably somewhere "south of Carnforth". Newby Bridge Halt was officially closed to passenger traffic on September 12th, 1939.

**Locomotives used on the Line, 1900-1939**

The 2-4-2Ts and their trains of six-wheeled coaches continued to handle local services on the branch, although in 1905 a steam railmotor was introduced in an effort to attract more passengers to the line. The vehicle was, in effect, a large bogie coach with a small, outside cylinder 0-4-0 locomotive built into one end, and a guard's compartment at the other end with accommodation for 48 passengers in the middle. The railmotor was finished in the standard blue and white Furness livery, and hauled a matching four-wheeled trailer. A similar vehicle was provided for service on the nearby Coniston branch, but both were withdrawn after a very short period. It is said that certain local businessmen complained that the 12-seater first class saloons were inadequate, but another reason for the early withdrawal of the two railmotors may have been poor availability—they were, after all, largely experimental machines, and when the engines needed attention the whole unit had to stay in the shops.

The old Sharp, Stewart 0-6-0s were replaced by more modern 0-6-0 tender engines during the present century. The new engines had been introduced in 1899, and have been designated the "D3" Class (the Furness had no regular system of class notation). 0-6-0 tank engines were also used on the branch freights, together with an occasional 0-6-2T which was usually "L2" No. 105. In 1915, the first two members of a class of 4-4-2T branch line engines were delivered from Kitson & Co. of Leeds. There were eventually six of these engines, numbered from 38 to 43, and they took over the Lakeside locals after the First World War. The regulars were Nos. 38 and 42, although Nos. 41 and 43 occasionally appeared.

The heavy excursion traffic was usually worked by 4-4-0s, 0-6-2Ts and 0-6-0s. The 4-4-0s were often members of the "K2" Class, introduced in 1896, but other types could sometimes be seen. Much of the excursion traffic originated on the Midland

and London & North Western systems and it was therefore quite common to see long trains of these companies' stock standing in the sidings at Lakeside, the dark purple-brown colours of the North Western contrasting with the red of the Midland and the blue-and-white of the local Furness trains—a colourful era indeed. These "foreign" trains were worked forward from the junction station at Carnforth by Furness engines; "D4" 0-6-0s Nos. 3 and 4 and "L2" class 0-6-2Ts Nos. 103 and 105 were regularly used on these workings. They would return light from Lakeside for use on other duties before returning later to work the return trips back to Carnforth.

It will be obvious from the above notes that the Lakeside line saw a considerable variety of motive power in pre-Grouping days, and this variety was to be a feature of the line throughout the L.M.S. and B.R. periods. The immediate post-Grouping period was a particularly interesting one for locomotive enthusiasts, as, for the first time, former Midland, North Western and even Lancashire & Yorkshire engines ran all the way to Lakeside. The Grouping did, unfortunately, result in a wholesale slaughter of many former Furness engines—the old 4-4-2Ts, for example, were all scrapped by 1932—but these losses were compensated for by the appearance of interesting "foreign" classes on local as well as excursion trains. Local passenger trains passed into the hands of ex-Lancashire & Yorkshire Railway 2-4-2 tanks, which were drafted onto the Furness system to replace the former F.R. branch line tanks. The L. & Y. engines were hardly young—in fact they had first been introduced back in 1889—but, as they belonged to a numerically large class, it was considered more efficient to use them than to retain the Furness engines. Nos. 10660, 10643 and 10646 were among those used on the line, and it is thought that, as they were the regular branch engines, one was usually shedded at Lakeside.

One Furness class seen in the 1930s was the famous "Baltic" 4-6-4 tank. Built by Kitson's the five members of this class had rarely, if ever, appeared on the Lakeside branch in F.R. days, but by the mid-30s, when they were no longer considered "top link" engines, they sometimes worked the branch locals (probably as replacements for failed L. & Y. 2-4-2Ts). No. 11103 appears to have been a fairly regular performer, until it was eventually withdrawn as the last survivor of the class in September 1940. By the late 1930s, standard L.M.S. types, such as the Stanier 2-6-4Ts, 4F 0-6-0s, and the "Black 5" 4-6-0s had started to appear on the branch, and these modern classes eventually replaced all the old pre-Grouping engines; indeed, the "Black 5s" were destined to work on the branch right up until its closure in 1965.

# 3. Nationalisation

As we have seen, the railway started to lose its passenger traffic in the 1930s, when rival forms of transport arrived on the scene. The "great depression", too, continued to affect both passenger and freight traffic; a major blow was caused by the closure of both Low Wood and Black Beck gunpowder works, although there was some consolation in the fact that, at about the same time, the Backbarrow Ironworks changed over from charcoal to coke fuel. In 1946 the summer-only passenger service was re-introduced, along with the Windermere steamer sailings. It was quite clear that the intermediate stations on the branch were now of little use, and the first sign of this was the closure, to passengers, of Greenodd and Haverthwaite on September 30th, 1946 (occasionally, however, special excursions picked up at Haverthwaite and Greenodd after this date). Trains continued to stop at Haverthwaite, but only for passing purposes; however, because of the heavy excursion traffic, the loop there was in constant use during the summer.

On January 1st, 1948, a nationwide fanfare of locomotive whistles welcomed the birth of British Railways. This change of ownership had little effect on the Lakeside branch, and the summer-only service continued as before—the only noticeable difference was the livery on the coaching stock, which changed from the maroon of the L.M.S. Railway to the striking red-and-cream of the new state-owned organisation. The petrol shortages of the "austerity" era meant that holidaymakers continued to flock to the Lake District by train, and the passenger timetable in force on the Lakeside line reflected the continued popularity of the railway and its associated steamers. The 1956 timetable, for example, provided good branch connections at Ulverston both out of, and into, Barrow and Morecambe trains—some of the latter, in fact, ran through to the terminus at Lakeside, the 09-50 from Euston Road taking 1 hour 39 minutes for the complete journey (including the Ulverston reversal). Through workings to and from Barrow were sparse, consisting of the 12-40 (SO) ex-Barrow and the 19-18 ex-Lakeside. At the height of the season there were four or five trains each way on the branch, although generally this was increased by excursion traffic from places other than Barrow or Morecambe.

This still quite extensive pattern of services enabled British Railways to continue to offer a variety of combined rail/water/road tours. To quote 1956 as an example once again, there were eight basic tours (and numerous permutations) giving holiday-makers an attractive choice of Lakeland trips. A typical tour of the 1950s—the "Windermere Circular"—took travellers from Morecambe or Lancaster to Lakeside by train. They then journeyed up to Ambleside by steamer, turned round, and voyaged back to Bowness, ready to return home by train from the former L. & N.W. station at Windermere Town; the fares for this delightful trip were still (to us in the inflation-ridden 'seventies) laughably cheap—10s. 9d. return from Morecambe or 10s. 6d. from Lancaster! (The return fare from Ulverston to Lakeside was only 2s.)

Locomotives seen on the branch in British Railways days were usually standard ex-L.M.S. classes, such as "Black 5" 4-6-0s, Stanier and Fairburn 2-6-4Ts and, on a less regular basis, "4F" 0-6-0s, "Patriot" 4-6-0s and Ivatt 2-6-0s. On June 6th, 1961, the branch had an unusual visitor in the shape of 4-6-2 No. 72003 "Clan Fraser" at the head of a special from Southport. The line did not normally play host to "foreign" motive power, but the 1961 summer appears to have been the exception to this, since there were several reports of Eastern Region B1 4-6-0s appearing at Lakeside on excursions from various parts of Yorkshire. The daily branch freight train was at this time handled by interesting motive power in the form of ex-Midland Railway 2F 0-6-0s; three or four of these ancient machines—which belonged to a class first introduced in 1875—were stationed at Barrow, and Nos. 58309, 58177 and 58287 were regular performers.

Yet, in spite of these interesting old engines and the fairly lavish passenger service still provided, there was no escaping the fact that the B.R. era on the branch was a time of decline, and that passenger loadings continued to fall year by year. However, B.R. was yet to adopt the concept of the "basic railway" and there was little evidence of physical rationalisation. The Leven curve, reinstated after the Second World War, was lifted for the third and final time in the late 1950s, the associated box at Greenodd Junction was taken out of use around the same time, and a number of sidings were removed from Haverthwaite yard—but otherwise facilities for traffic remained very much the same as they always had been. Lavish facilities for stabling excursion stock remained at Lakeside, and the branch was still worked in three sections: Plumpton Junction—Greenodd, Greenodd—Haverthwaite and Haverthwaite—Lakeside. The survival of Greenodd signal box until the branch finally closed to passenger traffic is curious, since its final role appears to have been merely as a block post on the Plumpton—Haverthwaite section; until the late 1950s, Greenodd was the station where the double line from Plumpton Junction became single for the rest of the way to Lakeside. After that time, single-line working was instituted between the junction and Greenodd, and the former down line (reduced to a long siding) used for storing surplus freight stock.

The slow decline continued throughout the 1950s and into the 1960s. With the increased affluence characteristic of a modern consumer society, more and more households gained access to a car, and this, above all else, is why the Lakeside branch lost its once-important passenger traffic. By the 1960s the road lobby had succeeded in diverting the lion's share of public investment in transport into roads and away from railways; at the same time the notorious Beeching Plan spelt out doom for local and branch railway services up an down the country—including the Lakeside line. The Beeching Plan, generally speaking, envisaged that railways carrying below 10,000 passengers a week would be closed, and maps, drawn up to indicate the density of traffic on B.R., purported to show which lines were profitable and which were not. As the number of passengers or tons of freight were calculated on the basis of traffic **passing over** the lines concerned, it is clear that "dead end" branches such as the Lakeside branch would appear to be carrying little traffic, whereas main lines would seem to be giving rise to a far greater proportion of goods and passengers; the fact that traffic could and did **originate** on a branch, and then flow onto a main line, was conveniently ignored. Hence, on the simplistic Beeching model, it could be argued that branch lines were un-economic, and should therefore be closed to save public money.

The Lakeside branch, which according to B.R. carried below 5,000 passengers a week, was therefore "under sentence of death" by the 1960s. In fact, it had been rumoured locally that the line would be closed at the end of the 1960 summer season, but in the event B.R. decided not to proceed further at that time. Indeed, far from closing the branch, a programme of heavy maintenance work was carried out. This included the re-laying of long stretches of the line with experimental concrete sleepers so that most B.R. locomotive classes (steam and diesel) would be allowed to work up to Lakeside. When the work was completed, a B.R. spokesman stated that the branch would last twenty years without major track renewals! The local "prophets of doom" were not, however, convinced, and in October 1964 their worst fears were realised when B.R. announced that passenger services would cease in the spring of 1965—which meant, in effect, that the line would simply not re-open for the 1965 steamer season on Windermere.

As objections to the closure had been received, the usual Transport Users' Consultative Committee enquiry took place at Ulverston on January 13th, 1965. In retrospect, it is now clear that these T.U.C.C. "enquiries" were mere formalities. Nevertheless, objectors often came up with ingenious arguments, and the Ulverston enquiry was no exception. One humorist quoted from the line's original Act of Parliament, which contained a clause stipulating that "the line shall be kept open **for all time** as far as Greenodd". This clause—which was included in the Act because the railway had meant the end of Greenodd's port facilities—was similar to one inserted into the Act of the Lewes & East Grinstead Railway in Sussex, which promised that trains would run "for evermore". In the case of the Lewes & East Grinstead line, B.R. was forced to re-open the route after it had actually been closed. Unfortunately, B.R's lawyers were later able to circumvent this type of clause, and so the "for all time" argument could not save the Lakeside line. Another objector referred to a further Act of 1886, which stipulated that, in the event of closure, the railway company would have to re-instate the former opening span on the (main line) Leven Viaduct so that ships could sail up to Greenodd once again!

In contrast to these rather flippant objections, B.R's argument for closure was based on apparent cold logic; in the 1964 season, it was claimed, only 46,709 passengers travelled between Ulverston and Lakeside, while 49,569 were carried in the opposite direction. Therefore, it was argued, the branch was unprofitable. However, as at other T.U.C.C. enquiries, the economics of running the branch were examined **in isolation** from the rest of the system; the fact that the 96,278 passenger journeys made on the line brought revenue to other stations (such as Barrow and Morecambe) was ignored. So, too, was the line's freight traffic, which surely paid for the costs of track maintenance. When objectors tried to raise this point at T.U.C.C. enquiries, they were automatically ruled "out of order" by the chairman—for goods traffic was outside the scope of the T.U.C.C.

And so, despite last-minute appeals from public bodies such as Southport Corporation—which resented the fact that yet another Lakeland branch would no longer be available for special trains for the old and infirm—and Mr. Alfred Hall-Davies, the local M.P., who requested a one-year reprieve — closure became a certainty. A fortnight later the T.U.C.C. reported that only "limited hardship" would be caused by the loss of the service, and on July 6th the Minister of Transport announced that the line would close on September 6th, 1965, subject to the provision of additional Ribble 'bus services (since withdrawn). In view of the line's summer-only passenger service, it was perhaps true that the closure caused little hardship. However, as B.R. admitted, the losses (and therefore the savings) on the Lakeside line were only marginal, and as the line provided a useful feeder service it is possible that the closure did more harm than good. Looking back, it appears that the closure was forced through with indecent haste (particularly as B.R. had taken the decision at the same time to expand the Windermere steamer business as a major tourist attraction).

1965, then, was the final year in which the line operated as a nationalised passenger-carrying railway. During this final summer the majority of trains were formed of corridor stock, hauled by ex-L.M.S. engines (although the B.R. "Standard" types are known to have put in some appearances). The branch never became a diesel stronghold, although excursions originating in central or southern Lancashire were often handled by English Electric Type 4s (now Class 40) or else were composed of six or eight car d.m.u. sets. Since the Furness line was still a stronghold of steam, however, few local workings were diesel-hauled, and goods workings, which by this time ran on Mondays, Wednesdays and Fridays only, remained steam-worked until final closure in 1967. One diesel type which is known to have worked fairly regularly on the branch, however, was the "Metro Vick" Type 2 Co-Bo; known to drivers as "Wonderloafs", these unusual locomotives were one of the results of B.R's much-criticised policy of ordering diesels from an assortment of engineering industries, and were drafted on to the Furness line "en masse" in 1962 (this was presumably intended to be their last resting place, since the whole class had been withdrawn by 1968). As a result, they could often be seen on Barrow-Lakeside workings during the last two or three years of passenger traffic. The axe finally fell, as expected, at the end of the season, and the last train—the 19-45 d.m.u. from Lakeside—ran on September 5th, 1965. There were, sadly, no ceremonies to mark the end of nearly 100 years of passenger services.

Goods traffic between Plumpton Junction and Haverthwaite survived for another 19 months and indeed, was still quite heavy; the remaining four sidings in Haverthwaite goods yard continued to handle coal traffic, "blue" from the Backbarrow dyeworks, and coke and ore for the iron works; motive power in these last "twilight" days was usually an Ivatt 2-6-0. The end came in 1967, when the Charcoal Iron Company decided to close its Backbarrow works after a life of at least 280 years; with the cessation of its main source of traffic, the railway could not hope to survive and remaining freight services were withdrawn from April 24th, 1967. The branch fell into dereliction, and B.R. announced that the lifting of the track (which as we have seen, had only recently been relaid to full main line standards) was imminent. The Manchester Locomotive and Stephenson Locomotive Societies therefore decided to arrange what was to be positively **the last** train, and on September 2nd, 1967, a brakevan special headed by "Black 5" No. 45134 ventured onto the abandoned branch. On entering Haverthwaite, it was found that the road was set for the ironworks branch—which ends in a precipitous drop—and it was only through the highly dubious means of breaking into the signal box that the points could be changed! Heading into the gathering gloom, the special moved off up the 1 in 60 gradient out of Haverthwaite. At Lakeside, several people stopped and stared at the train as it ran into the now-closed station and prepared to run round; how many, one wonders, realised the significance of this, the last B.R. train to run up to the lake? No. 45134 coupled up to the brake vans once more, and then returned to Ulverston and Carnforth. Now the whole branch lay forlorn and abandoned, waiting the hammers and oxy-acetylene torches of the scrap men. . . .

# 4. Revival and Reopening (1967-1977)

IN April 1967 one of the authors of this book (Mr. H. I. Quayle) wrote a letter to the "Barrow News" stating that the Leven Valley line would be worth saving. He pointed out that the line ran through some extremely beautiful scenery, with views of the sea, rivers and mountains, and that, of course, it connected with the Windermere steamers at Lakeside. A line of such character, he argued, "should not be allowed to die". The letter-writer believed that he was merely a voice in the wilderness; however, unknown to him, there were others with similar aims and ideas, who were equally determined that the last surviving Furness branch should not go the way of its neighbours. In April, Dr. Peter Beet, a well-known local practitioner and railway enthusiast, had purchased Ivatt class 2MT 2-6-0 No. 46441 from B.R., and had begun to repaint the locomotive in Midland Railway "crimson lake" livery. Originally, it had been agreed to send No. 6441 (as it soon became known, even though it did not carry that number) to the Keighley & Worth Valley Railway, but by June 1967 the Lakeside Railway Estates Co. Ltd. had been formed and matters began to take on a new and more exciting complexion.

The aim of the newly-formed company was to re-open and operate the Lakeside branch in its entirety, primarily as a tourist attraction, although (in common with many other preservation schemes at that time) the prospectus proposed that "as time and conditions permit, a full commuter and freight-carrying service using steam and diesel traction will be instituted"! Although the Lakeside Railway Estates Company may not have been totally serious in putting forward these particular proposals, the Company's directors recognised the potential of the branch. A problem which lay ahead was the right of Local Authorities in the area to purchase portions of the line in absolute preference to any other bidder. However, British Rail recognised that the Company meant business, and the lifting of the branch, scheduled for September 1967, was postponed.

Meanwhile, the Lakeside Railway Society had been born; some seven years previously a group of enthusiasts had formed the

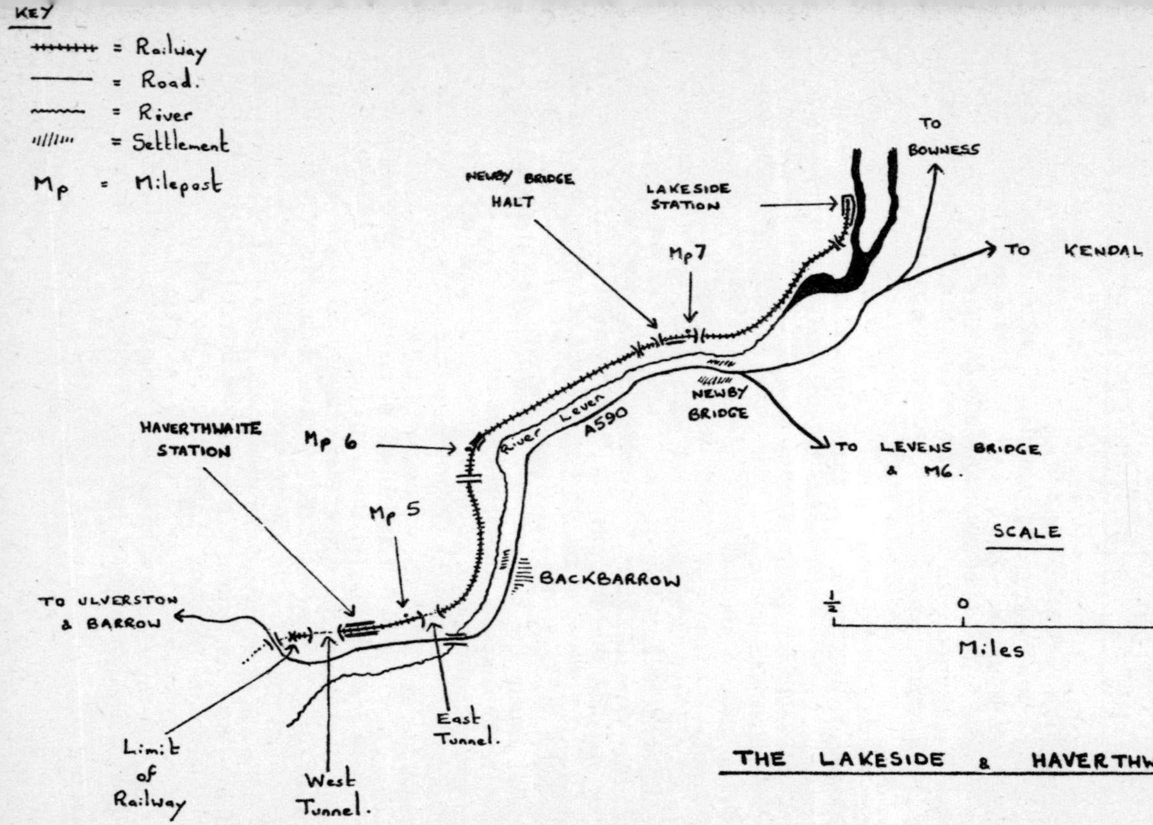


THE LAKESIDE & HAVERTHWAITE RAILWAY

Lancaster Railway Circle, and in 1967 this group approached the Company with a view to becoming a "supporters' group" for the Lakeside branch project. In June 1968 the Lancaster Railway Circle was re-formed and incorporated into the Lakeside Railway Society (L.R.S.). A further locomotive was then purchased by members of the L.R.S. from Courtauld's, Preston (Peckett No. 1925, named "Caliban"). 1967 closed with the Company in a favourable position with B.R. and the Ministry of Transport, but in January 1968 a major problem arose when the Lake District Planning Board decided to exercise its right to purchase the Lakeside to Haverthwaite section of the line for possible future conversion into a public footpath. In view of the considerable progress to date, this new proposal came as a serious blow, and both Company and Society were united in their determination to fight the Planning Board. There followed a considerable volume of correspondence between the parties concerned, and by the beginning of February 1968 the Society's secretary was able to report that he felt "the Lake District Planning Board were giving our proposals serious consideration and will listen to any sensible comment". In April, however, the Board affirmed its determination to proceed with the trackbed acquisition, and the fight began in earnest.

The Company sought legal advice in an attempt to stop the sale going through, while the Society opted for the equally effective step of organising a petition. By the end of May this had amassed some 5,000 signatures, with response being particularly encouraging in the Haverthwaite and Greenodd areas. Early in June the petition passed the 7,000 mark, and by late summer had levelled off at 12,600 signatures. This large body of support for the railway obviously influenced the Board, and in September 1968 a compromise proposal was put forward. This was based on an agreement between B.R., the Board and the Company, under which the Board agreed to purchase the trackbed for use as a footpath **and** a railway—the Board was to establish its footpath on one half of the double-track formation, and lease the remainder (on which the single-line railway stood) to the Company. This was a victory for common-sense, and the directors were able to write that "both interests are to be blended to the benefit of the public". Rather premature, however, in view of what was to come was the statement that "the preservation of the most beautiful branch in Great Britain is assured"!

Nonetheless, other events concerning the branch at this time were tending to support such comments. In January 1968 two Fairburn 2-6-4Ts (Nos. 42073 and 42085) were privately purchased with a view to their use on the branch; like No. 6441, they were members of a class which had seen service on the line in B.R. days and, like the red livery on the Ivatt engine, their proposed colour schemes were both unusual and controversial. No. 42073 was to appear in London & North Western black, while No. 42085 would sport Caledonian Railway blue, lined in black and white, and with deep red cylinders and frames. These two engines arrived at the Company's depot at Carnforth engine shed—some 17½ miles east of Plumpton—in the summer of 1968.

Membership of the Society continued to grow—aided, of course, by the almost hysterical level of interest engendered by the demise of steam on B.R. In May 1968 the members of the L.R.S. held a most successful meeting in the Swan Hotel at Newby Bridge, and during the course of this meeting the Society's first official committee was elected. Things were now beginning to move more quickly on the locomotive front. With the official end of steam on B.R. in August 1968, there was a great demand by preservation societies and private individuals for modern steam locomotives in good working order, and by the end of the year no less than six ex-L.M.S. "Black Five" 4-6-0s had arrived at Carnforth to join the 2-6-0 and the two 2-6-4Ts; the new engines were former B.R. Nos. 44871, 45231, 44767, 44806, 44932, and 45407.

In retrospect, 1968 had been a dynamic year for both the Company and the Society, and it is worthwhile quoting the following passage from the December 1968 edition of the L.R.S. journal "The Iron Horse": "... we have seen the society mature from a subsidiary of the Lancaster Railway Circle with a membership of 30 to a going concern with a membership of over 300 ... we have cleared our biggest obstacle, the Lake District Planning Board ... we have gained the support of all the local councils concerned, as well as the Lancashire County Council, and our latest step has left us with one foot in Carnforth Depot".

Then came 1969, a year that promised so much and yet gave so little.

**The Problem Era**

1969, the year in which the Lakeside branch was to celebrate its centenary, started well. Some 80% of the Society's members renewed their subscriptions, confident that wheels would soon be turning on the branch, while on April 1st the Lakeside Railway Estates Company became the official tenant of Carnforth motive power depot. Hopes ran high that Sunday, June 1st, the centenary day, would be celebrated by the running of steam specials on the branch—indeed, arrangements were drawn up for three specials to work up to Lakeside terminus. In the event, however, B.R. turned down these plans, although not before the matter had reached the ears of the highest authorities at Euston. On the other hand, this disappointment was somewhat tempered by the prospect of the first "open day" at Carnforth, scheduled

Furness Railway 2-4-2T No. 73 arrives at Ulverston station with the Lakeside branch train. This station was specially laid out to permit easy interchange between branch and main line trains. (Sankey Collection.)

0-6-0T No. 21 crosses Greenodd viaduct with a train from Lakeside. Like other photographs from the Sankey Collection, this view dates from the early years of this century.

Haverthwaite station, looking towards Lakeside. (Sankey Collection.)

An idyllic study of the small Newby Bridge Platform which has a charm all of its own. (Sankey Collection.)

The Morecambe-Lakeside "Lake Windermere Cruise" train at Newby Bridge behind 2-6-4T No. 42136 on June 17th, 1962. (Noel A. Machell.)

Metro-Vickers Co-Bo No. D5717 heads a return Lakeside-Birmingham excursion across Greenodd viaduct on June 2nd, 1963. (Noel A. Machell.)

Panoramic view of Lakeside station, and its magnificent background of lake and mountain, with a 5MT 4-6-0 on the "Lake Windermere Cruise" train. (Derek Cross.)

The diesel age comes to Lakeside, as a d.m.u. stands ready to convey guests to Barrow (Island Road) for the Vickers "1,000th diesel engine for British Railways" ceremony on October 16th, 1964. (R. A. Hope.)

for the same date, when Nos. 46441, 42073 and 44871 would be "on shed" and in steam. The open day was a great success, and over 3,000 visitors paid to walk round the Carnforth engine sheds; it seemed that the B.R. ban on the steam specials was only a minor ripple on an otherwise tranquil sea.

Unfortunately, this same summer of 1969 saw the Lancashire County Council proposing "improvements" to the A590 Levens Bridge to Barrow trunk road—and these "improvements" would have the effect of truncating the Lakeside branch just south of Haverthwaite and again at Greenodd. Because of this, the Company issued a statement on September 21st pointing out that "a request has been made to the British Railways Board to apply to the Minister of Transport for a Light Railway Order for the section Haverthwaite to Lakeside, and for permission to deliver as soon as possible to that section certain items of stock and equipment". The statement stressed, however, that the Company was still hopeful of resolving the difficulties over the remainder of the branch. Obviously, supporters of the scheme still hoped that the entire route could be saved, and they received valuable backing from local papers such as the "Barrow News" which considered the matter important enough to devote an editorial to it in November. In its opinion, "the Lakeside line was so valuable an asset that it should never have been closed". A steam railway running all the way from Ulverston to Lakeside, continued the paper, would be "a tremendous tourist attraction" for the area. Others, however, thought otherwise, and rumours began to circulate to the effect that the preservation of the branch was about to collapse. These rumours culminated in the publication of a news item in the "Railway Magazine", which claimed that the Company had no further interest in the branch and that no more negotiations would be conducted with B.R. It appeared to the supporters of the project that all the hard work of the past 2½ years had been in vain.

Yet, although the "Railway Magazine" statement appeared to sound the death-knell of the branch, the reality of the situation was much more encouraging. In January 1970 the directors of the Company had split into two separate camps, with one group aiming to promote Carnforth motive power depot and the other deciding to concentrate on the Lakeside branch project. Thus, the Lakeside & Haverthwaite Railway Company Ltd. was born, and the energetic directors of the new Company quickly began to re-open negotiations with B.R. The Society continued to back both the Carnforth and the branch projects, but a growing number of members felt that a decision should be made to support the branch project only. By mid-June the "split" between the two projects had become official, and the Lakeside Railway Estates Company wrote to the secretary of the Society indicating that there could be no more working parties at Carnforth and stating that all property belonging to the L.R.S. would have to be moved within one month.

There was little regret among Society members, especially as B.R. had now granted the L.R.S. limited access to the branch at Haverthwaite station. Initially, this was for the sole purpose of weeding and tidying-up, but, in practice, wheels were soon turning on the branch once again in the form of the Society's small Wickham petrol trolley and trailer. This humble vehicle, which had lain derelict at Clapham (Yorkshire) for five years before the L.R.S. purchased it, was to prove invaluable during the first "low-profile" stages of restoration. The Society continued to tidy-up the Haverthwaite site throughout the summer of 1970, and by so doing aroused considerable interest among local people and tourists alike. Meanwhile, the L. & H.R. Company was scouring the country for suitable rolling stock. Eventually, seven B.R. Mk. I coaches (Nos. E24377, E24248, E24381, E24731, E24449, E24799 and E34181) and an ex-L.N.E.R. full brake, built in 1936 (No. E70361E), were purchased from the Eastern Region and placed in store at York until B.R. could authorise stock movements onto the branch. During the next few months, contracts were drawn up between B.R. and the L. & H.R., and on September 9th—some three years after the S.L.S. "Last Train"—Class 25 Diesel No. D7556 travelled up the weed-grown branch with a track-testing train. The journey to Haverthwaite was accomplished in 40 minutes, and on arrival the B.R. Inspector announced that he was satisfied with the test, and that it would be possible to move the L. & H.R. rolling stock over the abandoned lower portion of the line.

The first (and probably the most important) stock movement took place on Wednesday, October 14th. That grey day was destined to be one which both Society and Company would never forget. The proceedings began on the other side of the Pennines at 03-30 hrs. in the morning, when Class 24 No. D5100 headed the 8X82 Special for Haverthwaite out of York North Yard. This was, of course, formed of the L. & H.R's carriage stock, and after a leisurely journey over the Pennines the train made a breakfast stop at Carnforth (Furness & Midland Junction) at 07-20. Plumpton Junction was reached at 09-44, and it is interesting to record that the Class 24 used part of the old Conishead Priory Branch (see below) as a headshunt during its reversal operations; this was probably the first time that passenger vehicles had traversed its metals since it closed to passengers some 54 years previously! Haverthwaite yard was gained at 10-50, and the crew of the special were treated to a fresh brew of tea on arrival. After positioning the coaches in the goods roads (which were, of course, no longer needed for goods traffic as such), the Class 24 set off back to the West Riding.

As No. D5100 passed Carnforth, it was saluted by a blast on the horn of 0-6-0 diesel shunter No. D3200, which stood at the head of the second Society special of the day—"The Lakeside & Haverthwaite Harbinger". This consisted of the two Fairburn 2-6-4Ts, together with "Caliban" (see above), and the Society's riding van (i.e. mess van). Heading down the Furness main line at a steady 15 m.p.h., the train reached Plumpton Junction by mid-afternoon. Dozens of cameras clicked as the special reversed and then set off along the branch. Those Society members lucky enough to be on board savoured the experience of travelling over the doomed lower portion of the branch, almost certainly for the very last time. All too soon the "Harbinger" reached Haverthwaite and, after positioning No. 42085 in the goods shed—which made an excellent engine shed—the diesel shunter returned to Carnforth.

The following month it was the turn of the Society's and Company's freight stock. This time the special train was worked from Barrow Yard to Haverthwaite behind another Class 08 diesel, No. D4118, and the stock moved up included two box vans, a bogie bolster, an open wagon and a flat wagon, together with "Fluff", the Society's tiny 0-4-0 diesel shunting locomotive. On November 26th a further stock movement took place when Stanier Class 5 4-6-0 No. 44806 was moved from Accrington to Haverthwaite. Two weeks previously a low loader had rolled into Haverthwaite yard bearing two small Hudswell-Clarke saddle tanks.

B.R., which had put its plans for track-lifting into cold storage since 1967, was by now indicating that it would like to recover the metals on the lower section of the line, and the Company therefore made hurried arrangements for the final stock movements to take place early in 1971. At the end of April that year, Class 25 No. D7554 worked up from Plumpton with a tank wagon—which had been kindly donated by the Esso Petroleum Co.—and on May 7th, 1971, the arrival at Haverthwaite of Brake Second Open coach No. E9218 behind Class 25 No. D5194 marked the end of an era. A few weeks later the demolition contractors moved in, and by the end of June the Lakeside & Haverthwaite Railway had been cut off for ever from the national rail system.

There were now six steam locomotives, one diesel, nine passenger vehicles, a riding van, and six goods wagons at Haverthwaite. Subsequent arrivals included an ex-L.M.S. goods brake van, Class 03 diesel shunter No. 2117 and "Princess", a Bagnall 0-6-0 saddle-tank locomotive. There was therefore plenty of work for the Sunday working parties—which averaged 31 throughout 1971. Besides restoration and preparation work on the locomotives and rolling stock, the Sunday volunteers managed to clear vegetation from the track, erect a fence around the locomotive compound at Haverthwaite, install a buffer stop at the recently severed "end of the line", and drop and grease every fishplate on the line! A notable achievement concerned the old halt at Newby Bridge which, after 30 years of neglect, was literally buried under mounds of earth and rubbish; after a mammoth clearing-up operation the halt finally emerged as good as new!

Negotiations over the line's re-opening, which was dependent on the granting of a Light Railway Order by the Ministry of Transport, dragged on—not helped by the lengthy postal strike during the early part of 1971. In private, the directors now believed that full public services would not start until the spring of 1972. During the Easter weekend of 1971, however, following extensive press advertising, many holidaymakers turned up to view the static displays at Haverthwaite, and on Friday, May 7th, steam returned to the branch at last when "Caliban" headed the first steam-hauled works train up the line, having successfully passed her "in steam" boiler examination that very morning. "Caliban" was steamed again on the following Sunday, when it hauled No. 42073 up to Lakeside to be watered—for Haverthwaite was not yet connected to the mains; "Caliban" then returned to Haverthwaite to collect a track-clearance gang, and thereby enabled the "rank-and-file" of the L.R.S. to have a ride up to Newby Bridge behind a steam engine! By the end of the month, Society members could once again sample the delights of steam haulage, for B.R. had given permission for "timetable trials" (in connection with the Windermere steamers) to take place; Nos. 42073 and 44806 therefore had their first opportunity in two years to show their paces. It began to look as if the beginning of scheduled steam-hauled services was not far off, and interest in getting the branch ready for that occasion was running high.

October 1971, just twelve months after the bulk of the locomotives and stock had moved to Haverthwaite, was another momentous month. The Company announced that negotiations for the line had been completed with the British Railways Property Board, and that Part I of the Light Railway Order required to re-open the branch had been applied for. All seemed set for re-opening, and the requisite legal announcements were put into the local newspapers in March 1972. However, one of the purposes behind making such announcements was to ascertain whether there were any objections to the proposed re-opening, and unfortunately there were—albeit of a minor nature. The chances of public-carrying steam trains to Lakeside by Easter 1972 were fast receding, although the delay did give the Society the opportunity of completing several jobs which, in any case, would have been required by the Department of the Environment's Inspecting Officer of Railways.

For some people, Friday the 13th has always been regarded as an unlucky day. For the supporters of the L. & H.R., however, Friday, October 13th, 1972, was one of the most memorable days ever, since it was on that day that the D.O.E. granted the British Railways Board the first part of the relevant Light Railway Order. For those unfamiliar with the legal aspects of the situation, it may be worth pointing out that Part I enabled B.R. to re-open the line as a light railway, but further legal agreement was now required between the B.R.B. and the L. & H.R. Company to enable the latter to run a train service. For the second time, therefore, notices had to be placed in all local newspapers for the benefit of would-be objectors, and once again both Society and Company waited with bated breath as the December 1st, 1972, deadline for such objections drew near. The wait, however, was not spent in idleness, for during this period B.R. gave permission for the L. & H.R. to run crew-training specials. This, in turn, provided the line's operating authorities with the opportunity of holding a further set of timetable trials, the results of which needed to be made available as soon as possible so that both the L. & H.R. and Sealink could begin to plan their publicity for the coming season.

December 1st came and went, and this time there were no objections; the line would at last be open in 1973! To many Society members—the "inspired amateurs" who had given so much time to the venture—the ending of the old year provided an opportunity for looking back on the intensive and sometimes seemingly unrewarding efforts of the past two years. Visions of the early days came flooding back—weeding parties in flaming June; track-clearance work up the line, and long, leisurely rides back to Haverthwaite on trains piled high with cut foliage; the autumn gloom descending on silent locomotives at Haverthwaite; the day "Fluff" lost part of her motion up by the lake, and was left marooned with only the moorhens for company; and the great revival of steam in the spring of 1971. Whatever the future might bring, to those stalwarts who had "seen it all" there was no denying the pleasures of the past.

**Opening and Beyond**

Early in 1973 the L. & H.R. published its first timetable. This advertised weekend services beginning on May 5th, and leading on to a seven-day-a-week timetable from May 20th until October 7th. There were to be six trains daily in each direction, rising to eight at the height of the season, and the journey time between Lakeside and Haverthwaite would be 18 minutes. The final legal hurdle was cleared in March 1973, when the ever-helpful Major Olver, the D.O.E's Inspecting Officer of Railways, made his final examination of the route. The L. & H.R. was now legally empowered to work the line, and the official re-opening was celebrated on Wednesday, May 2nd, 1973, with the Rt. Rev. Eric Treacy, the then Bishop of Wakefield, as the guest of honour.

The ceremony—which was a conscious echo of the great days of railway building a century before—began at Lakeside at 13-30 in the afternoon. A large crowd had gathered on both platforms to witness this historic event, and the two Fairburn tank engines stood ready to head the re-opening special down the line. Standing on the footplate of No. 42085, the Bishop gave a brief but witty speech and then cut the tape which had been slung between the engine and the platform. The four coach, double-headed special then drew away, whistling loudly in answer to the cheers from the crowd. All down the line, well-wishers had gathered to cheer and take photographs as the train threaded its way along the valley. A stop was made at Newby Bridge Halt, and Bishop Treacy climbed down onto the platform to plant a beech tree and unveil a commemorative plaque. On arrival at Haverthwaite another large crowd, which included 160 children from Backbarrow Primary School, had gathered to welcome the special and its passengers. After another quick turnround the train returned to Lakeside, where the official party transferred to M.V. "Swan" for a cruise on the lake—a pleasant reminder of the close links which still existed between the railway and the "steamers".

At 15-30 another special left Lakeside behind the Fairburn tanks—this time it was the turn of the officials and guests of the Lakeside Railway Society to enjoy a ride. The train returned to Lakeside behind 4-6-0 No. 44806, and then made three more return trips behind the big tender engine. Finally, the last train of the day was worked by the saddle tanks "Caliban" and "Princess", thus giving the railway's smallest locomotives the opportunity to show their paces on the steep climb out of Haverthwaite. All in all it had been quite a day, but, as one Society official was heard to remark, now that the celebrations were over it was time to "get down to the nitty-gritty of running a railway!"

There was indeed plenty of work still to be done. The coaching stock, for example, was still running in a B.R.-derived maroon livery without lining but with an "L.H.R." monogram at waist level; it was hoped, eventually, to devise a new livery, possibly based on an experimental colour scheme tried out on the B.S.O. (the suggested colours—red and cream—harked back to the B.R. livery seen on the branch in the 1950s). On the locomotive front, No. 44806 was christened "Magpie" by Susan Stranks of Thames Television on August 1st, 1973 (this engine has since been moved to Southport). In September that same year, an 0-6-0ST of the Hunslet Austerity variety arrived on a low loader, having been purchased from the Ministry of Defence at Shoeburyness, Essex. In May 1974 this locomotive was named "Cumbria" by Councillor Westoll, the chairman of the County Council.

The 1974 timetable provided for a slightly shorter operating season than before. On weekdays there were seven trains each way (rising to eight in high season), but on Saturdays there were only five trains each way. The majority of these workings were timed to connect with the Windermere steamers, which were obviously benefiting from their renewed railway link; a combined railway/steamer ticket—unique among British preserved railways—was available for travellers wishing to go from Haverthwaite to Bowness or Ambleside without re-booking. A further refinement, introduced in subsequent years, has been the combined rail, road and steamer tours, which continue the traditions built up by Aslett in Furness Railway days; however, whereas in the old days the railway company was the main organiser, today's combined tours are usually made possible through the enterprise of private coach tour operators. On the other hand a new type of rail-orientated tour, unknown in Aslett's day, has developed in more recent times; with the demise of steam on B.R., interest in steam-hauled specials has grown, and there have been several enthusiasts' specials over the Furness main line incorporating 'bus trips to the L. & H.R. These trips can bring welcome extra trade to the Lakes line; for example, in June 1975, over 600 enthusiasts visited the L. & H.R. as part of a steam rail tour from Leeds organised by the Keighley & Worth Valley Railway.

**The Future**

Will the L. & H.R. survive to see its 200th anniversary? Will steam trains continue to puff up the 1 in 60 to Linsty Green? Will the children of the 1970s, brought up in a steamless Britain, react to the sight of steam power in action in the same way as their parents? No one as yet knows the answer to these questions, which must also apply to other preserved lines. It is clear, however, that the L. & H.R. is in a better position than some other preserved lines; its locomotives and rolling stock, for example, are of modern design, and therefore need rather less maintenance than older equipment (some preserved lines are still using trains built in Queen Victoria's day!). Moreover, there is no doubt that tourism in English Lakeland will continue to benefit the railway by guaranteeing a steady flow of passenger traffic—again, the L. & H.R. is in a better position than some other lines, which are not lucky enough to be in recognised tourist areas. Let us hope, then, that the Lakeside & Haverthwaite Railway will steam on into the 21st century, and that its trains will continue to run through one of the loveliest valleys in England!

## LAKESIDE AND HAVERTHWAITE RAILWAY: LOCOMOTIVES

| *LHR No.* | *Previous No(s).* | *Name* | *Description* | *Date built* | *Builders* | *Where built* | *Driving wheel diameter* | *Cylinders* | *Tractive effort* | *Previous owners* |
|---|---|---|---|---|---|---|---|---|---|---|
| 1 | — | *Caliban* | 0-4-0ST (industrial) | 1937 | Pecket & Sons. | Bristol | 3′ 10″ | 16″ × 24″ | 20,435 lbs | Courtaulds, Preston |
| 2 | — | *Fluff* | 0-4-0DM 44 bhp | 1937 | Hunslet/Fowler | Leeds | — | — | — | Barrow Steelworks |
| 2073 | 42073 | — | Fairburn Class 4MT 2-6-4T | 1950 | British Rail (Southern Region) | Brighton | 5′ 9″ | $19\frac{5}{8}$″ × 26″ | 24,670 lbs | British Rail |
| 2085 | 42085 | — | Fairburn Class 4MT 2-6-4T | 1951 | British Rail (Southern Region) | Brighton | 5′ 9″ | $19\frac{5}{8}$″ × 26″ | 24,670 lbs | British Rail |
| 5 | 5,65 | — | 0-6-0ST (industrial) | 1929 | Hudswell-Clarke | Leeds | 3′ 4″ | 15″ × 22″ | 18,934 lbs | Appleby-Frodingham Steel Co |
| 6 | 76,6 | Renishaw Ironworks No. 6 | 0-6-0ST (industrial) | 1919 | Hudswell-Clarke | Leeds | 3′ 4″ | 15″ × 22″ | 18,934 lbs | Appleby-Frodingham Steel Co |
| 44806 | 4806, 44806 | — | Stanier Class 5MT 4-6-0 | 1944 | London, Midland & Scottish Railway | Derby | 6′ 0″ | $18\frac{1}{2}$″ × 28″ | 25,455 lbs | British Rail |
| 8 | D2117, 2117 | — | Class 03 0-6-0DM | 1959 | British Rail (Western Region) | Swindon | 3′ 7″ | — | 15,650 lbs | British Rail |
| 9 | — | *Rachel* | Four-wheeled tramway locomotive | 1924 | Motor Rail & Tram Car Company | Bedford | — | — | — | James Cropper & Co Ltd, Kendal |
| 14 | 14 | *Princess* | 0-6-0ST (industrial) | 1942 | W. G. Bagnall | Stafford | 3′ 6″ | 16″ × 24″ | 22,382 lbs | Preston Corporation |
| 94 | WD149 | Cumbria | 0-6-0ST (industrial) | 1953 | Hunslet | Leeds | 4′ 3″ | 18″ x 26″ | 23,870 lbs | M.O.D. Shoeburyness |

Since this list was compiled, No. 44806 has left the railway. An addition to the stock is LHR No. 11 (previous No. 3698) *Repulse*, built 1950 and previously owned by N.C.B. North-West (other details as "Cumbria", which is now LHR No. 10).

**LAKESIDE AND HAVERTHWAITE RAILWAY: CARRIAGES**

| *L & HR No.* | *BR No.* | *Description* | *Classification* | *Builders* | *Date built* |
|---|---|---|---|---|---|
| 40 | E24248 | BR 'Standard' Mark 1 second-class corridor carriage seating 64 | SK | BR, York | 1953 |
| 41 | E24377 | ditto | SK | Birmingham Railway Carriage and Wagon Company | 1953 |
| 42 | E24381 | ditto | SK | ditto | 1953 |
| 43 | E24449 | ditto | SK | BR, Swindon | 1954 |
| 44 | E24731 | ditto | SK | BR, Wolverton | 1953 |
| 45 | E24799 | ditto | SK | Birmingham Railway Carriage and Wagon Company | 1954 |
| 70 | E34181 | BR 'Standard' Mark 1, second-class corridor carriage seating 24, with brake and guard's and luggage compartments | BSK | BR, Wolverton | 1951 |
| 71 | E70361 | LNER Gresley-designed parcels van and brake, with guard's compartment | BG | LNER, York | 1936 |
| 72 | — | Riding van, with brake (formerly a Midland Railway clerestory-roofed compartment carriage) | — | MR, Derby | 1913 |
| 73 | E9218 | BR 'Standard' Mark 1 second-class open saloon carriage seating 39, with brake and guard's and luggage compartments | BSO | BR, Doncaster | 1953 |

# 5. The Route Described

HAVING examined the history of the railway itself, it is perhaps appropriate to describe the line in detail. The following chapter therefore takes the reader on an "armchair journey" along the Lakeside branch, starting at Ulverston—the one time "junction" for Lakeside trains. (The journey falls naturally into three parts; first, the still-extant main line section from Ulverston to Plumpton Junction; second, the now abandoned lower half of the line; and finally, the L. & H.R. proper, from Haverthwaite to Lakeside.)

**The Main Line Section: Ulverston to Plumpton Junction**

Ulverston — the "junction" for the Lakeside line — is the principal intermediate station on the southern section of the former Furness Railway main line. As we have seen the railway first reached the town in 1854, when the F.R. opened its line from Barrow. This first line terminated in a station facing on to what is now Springfield Road, and when, in 1857, the rails were carried eastwards by the Ulverston & Lancaster Railway, a new platform was constructed to the south of the old station, and the original station became an enlarged goods yard. Tickets were issued in the old station until the present passenger station was erected in 1873. Situated on a second new platform, it is an imposing building of red sandstone, two storeys high, and with a large clock tower.

The platform arrangements at Ulverston are unusual, but not quite unique, as a similar example could be found at Ventnor on the Isle of Wight Railway. The "up" platform is an island between the "up" and "down" lines, and this means that the "down" side has two platform faces! Through trains from Barrow to Lakeside would depart from the "up" side, but Ulverston to Lakeside locals used the "down" side; on arrival from Lakeside, the branch engine would run round its train and then rejoin the "up" line via the crossover at the eastern end of the station. This crossover—which survived the closure of the branch by several years—was worked by a ground frame released from Ulverston signal box.

Ulverston station has changed little over the years, and present-day travellers, sitting in the trains that continue to call here, can still see the Furness Railway monogram cast in the spandrels of the glass and iron platform canopies. The offices of the old station are now used by the local co-operative society, while the goods yard still contains several wagons and tankers. The station's continued survival is a reflection of the lack of road communication between Ulverston and the settlements to the east of the Leven estuary, and large numbers of workers and schoolchildren are carried daily to and from Ulverston by the morning and evening trains.

Leaving Ulverston the line enters a cutting, which however soon gives way to a tall embankment that dominates the eastern parts of Ulverston. In steam days the sight of Barrow-bound freights labouring up the 1 in 70 gradient to Lindal summit was a spectacular (but little-recorded) visual experience. The view from the embankment is itself quite spectacular; the grey stone town of Ulverston can be seen spread out to the north, with the 435 ft. high Hoad Hill beyond. Hoad Hill is topped by what appears to be a lighthouse, and the traveller, who may know something of Ulverston's maritime traditions, may be forgiven for thinking that the 100 ft. high monument was put there to guide homeward-bound vessels. In fact the "lighthouse" is a sham, and was erected in 1850 to commemorate Sir John Barrow, who was then Ulverston's most famous son. Sir John was born in a little whitewashed cottage—which can still be seen at Dragley Beck, to the south of the railway—in 1764, and, after an education in the town's grammar school, he went on to become a famous explorer, visiting such then little-known places as China, South Africa and the Arctic. He became Secretary of the Admiralty—a post which he held for forty years—and it was during this period that he wrote a standard work on the celebrated *Bounty* mutiny. The Victorians loved great men, although we tend to play them down; hence Sir John has a great monument (some might call it vulgar), but, apart from a recently-unveiled plaque, a more recent famous man is uncommemorated. It may come as a surprise to learn that Stan Laurel, the English half of the Laurel and Hardy comedy team, was born in Union Street—in a humble terraced house beneath the shadow of the Hoad.

Some ¾-mile from Ulverston station a substantial limestone and sandstone viaduct takes the railway over the Ulverston Canal. The canal was engineered by John Rennie and opened in 1796. Said to be the "straightest, shortest, deepest, widest canal in England", the waterway enabled vessels of up to 350 tons to sail right up to the town, and a small maritime colony grew up at Canal Head beneath the "lighthouse". Although the coming of the railway signalled the eventual extinction of the canal, the Furness company bought the waterway in 1862 and laid down an extensive system of sidings on its banks. These sidings ran from what became the Conishead Priory branch, which was itself joined to the main line at Plumpton Junction; Lakeside-bound travellers could look to their right as their train crossed the canal, and see in the distance the bridge which carried the Priory branch over the waterway. The canal was last used in about 1916, but most of the Priory branch and the sidings lasted until the 1960s and served several local industries. Indeed, a sizeable "stub" still runs from Plumpton Junction to the Glaxo chemical plant, which was opened in 1948 and is now one of the largest antibiotics plants in the world. The Glaxo plant is a striking, if ugly, addition to the landscape, but as Plumpton Junction is approached magnificent views of the Bleasdale Fells can be seen to the north, with the Trough of Bowland visible across the wide expanse of Morecambe Bay.

In spite of its completely rural location, the large signal box at Plumpton Junction reflects its former importance; it once controlled not only the Lakeside and Conishead Priory branches, but also an extensive system of running loops and the sidings which once ran into Plumpton Quarry. The importance of Plumpton Junction has, of course, diminished in recent years, and many of the levers in the box are now painted white, indicating that they are no longer used. The box remains a block post, however, and the canal branch still provides some activity in the one remaining loop; in recent years, chemical tank wagons have been taken along the branch to the Glaxo plant on Saturdays and Mondays and collected on Mondays, Wednesdays and Fridays.

**The Abandoned Plumpton—Haverthwaite Section**

The Lakeside branch diverged to the left and entered a shallow cutting as it began to curve round to the north. The double line passed beneath a road overbridge shortly after leaving the junction, and soon reached Greenodd Junction—the northern end of the "Leven Curve", used by through trains from Lancashire and West Yorkshire. A second overbridge spanned the cutting immediately beyond the junction, and the line then ran dead straight across the flat, reclaimed moss lands, with a low range of hills dominating the eastern horizon. After about a mile the trains passed a farm on the right-hand side of the line, and it was this farm that gave rise to the only level crossing on the branch—generally known as Plumpton Crossing.

As the trains approached Greenodd, the broad Leven estuary opened up on the right, and one of the finest "through the window" views in England revealed itself to the discerning traveller; against an impressive backdrop of green fells and rugged mountains, the tidal waters of the Leven ebbed and flowed beneath an

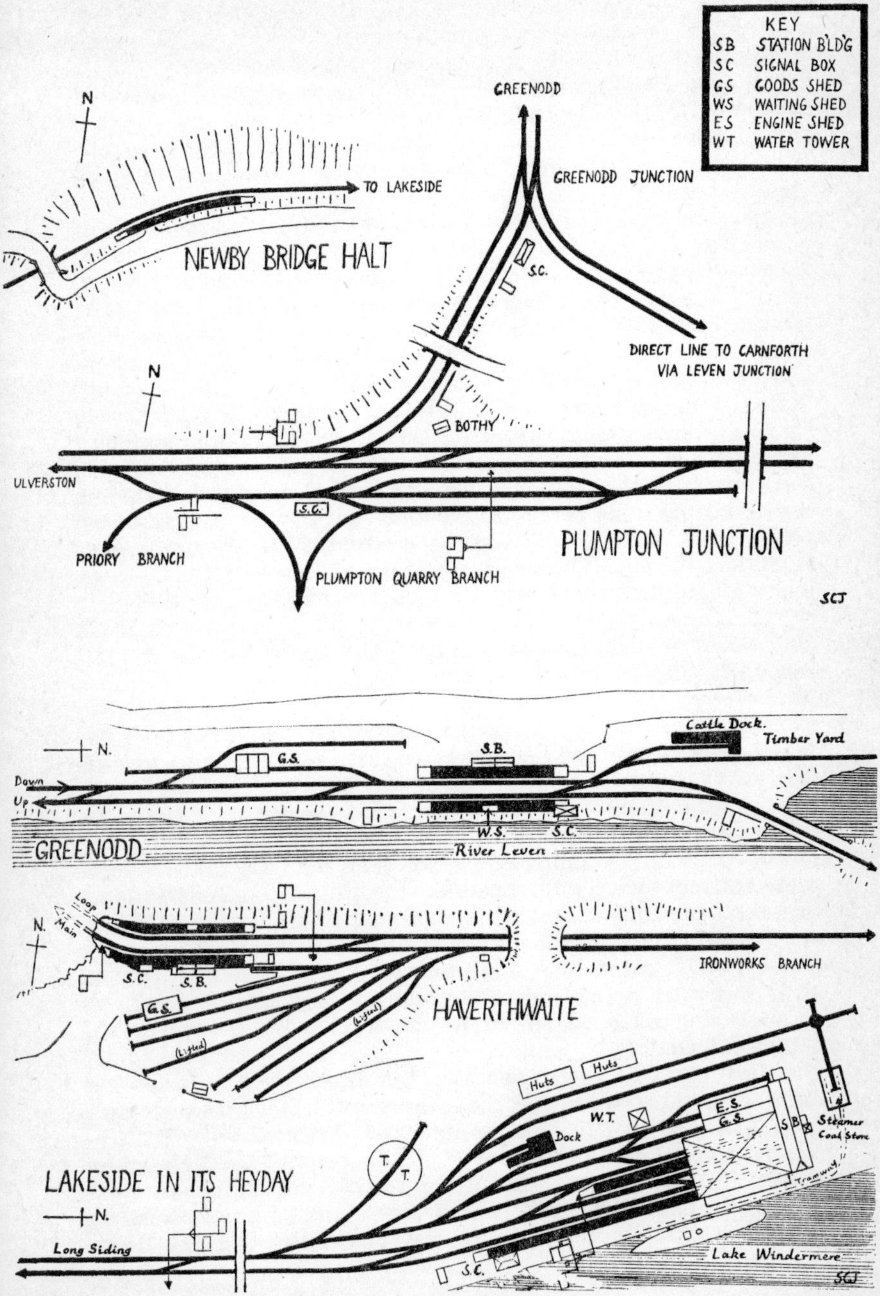
KEY
SB STATION B'LD'G
SC SIGNAL BOX
GS GOODS SHED
WS WAITING SHED
ES ENGINE SHED
WT WATER TOWER
N
TO LAKESIDE
NEWBY BRIDGE HALT
GREENODD
GREENODD JUNCTION
S.C.
DIRECT LINE TO CARNFORTH
VIA LEVEN JUNCTION
N
BOTHY
ULVERSTON
S.C.
PRIORY BRANCH
PLUMPTON QUARRY BRANCH
PLUMPTON JUNCTION
SCJ
N.
Cattle Dock.
Timber Yard
S.B.
G.S.
Down
Up
W.S.
S.C.
GREENODD
River Leven
Loop
Main
N.
S.C.
S.B.
G.S.
(Lifted)
(Lifted)
HAVERTHWAITE
IRONWORKS BRANCH
Huts
Huts
E.S.
G.S.
S.B.
W.T.
Steamer
Coal Store
Dock
T.T.
Tramway
LAKESIDE IN ITS HEYDAY
N.
Long Siding
S.C.
Lake Windermere
SCJ

ever changing sky which cast gigantic cloud-patterns on both river and mountains. To the north-east of this great vista, a cleft in the hills marked the gap through which the upper reaches of the river flowed down from Windermere—a gap which would be penetrated by the train on its climb up to the lake. To the left, tantalising glimpses could be obtained of the steeply-wooded Crake Valley as it wound its way up to Coniston Lake—only 4½ miles away.

Greenodd station, some two miles from Plumpton Junction, was perched right on the edge of the estuary, and at high tide the water lapped up right behind the up platform—a picturesque setting, but one which caused a tragedy in the early 1900s when the stationmaster's wife and his two children were drowned while picnicking near the station. The branch became single immediately beyond the platforms, and then curved to the east and crossed the Leven on a cast-iron viaduct. The goods yard, served by two sidings, was situated on the down side at the southern end of the platforms, while two further sidings ran off from the other end of the station—one terminated in an end-loading dock, and the other served a riverside timber yard. The standard yellow-brick station buildings were situated on the down platform, and the signal box and a waiting shelter were built on the up side—the latter had windows on all sides so that travellers could view the fine scenery while waiting for their trains. In its Edwardian heyday, Greenodd station had a staff of three porter-signalmen and one stationmaster, together with two platelayers who lived in the village.

This little riverside settlement was once a flourishing port, for in pre-railway days the Leven was an important routeway serving the area's numerous local industries; timber, charcoal, slate, copper, lead, gunpowder and other goods were shipped from as far upstream as Haverthwaite, and Greenodd itself had a flourishing shipbuilding industry (as we shall see, the first Windermere steamers were built here). By the time the railway opened, however, the importance of the Leven had declined, and when the Furness built its embankments across the mouth of the river Crake (which enters the Leven here) the final blow was dealt to both water transport and shipbuilding in the area—the railway builders did not even bother to construct a lifting span in the Greenodd viaduct.

Clattering across the viaduct, the trains ran onto a long embankment thrown across the estuary and headed towards Lady Syke Cottages—a pair of semi-detached Victorian villas built by the railway in the same "patent white bricks" used elsewhere on the line. To the left, the A590—the old pre-railway turnpike road from Greenodd to Levens Bridge—could be seen sneaking round the promontory of Legbarrow Point. Heading east-north-east, the single track railway crossed the river a second time on another girder bridge, which, like the Greenodd bridge, was built for a double line of rails. The branch to the Black Beck gunpowder works diverged to the left immediately beyond the bridge, and disappeared mysteriously into a distant plantation. There were at one time two dead end sidings here, but, as there was no run-round loop, gunpowder vehicles bound for Black Beck had to be placed in front of the locomotive at Greenodd and propelled up to the junction. (Further details of Dixon's Siding will be found in chapter 7.)

With the Leven now on the right hand side, the line started to climb towards Haverthwaite on a 1 in 80 gradient and entered a more enclosed, secluded section of the valley. After a mile or so the valley opened out again and the trains were carried above the slate-built village of Haverthwaite on an embankment. The dark houses and cottages with their thick walls and low-pitched roofs tended to look rather dour and gloomy, especially in the wet Lakeland weather, which only accentuated the blackness of their walls. A few, however, were rendered with plaster and whitewash, and on a summer afternoon these could provide a pleasant contrast to the radiant green of the valley. An overbridge carried the railway over a minor road (the B5278) near Haverthwaite post office, and then, still climbing at 1 in 80, the trains thundered beneath two overbridges, one of which carried a farm track while the other took the busy A590 across the line. St. Anne's church could be seen to the right before the rails plunged into the 165 yard long Haverthwaite West tunnel. The neat stone façade of the west portal was deceptive, as the tunnel was unlined apart from a short bricked section near the entrance. An eerie, dripping place, the tunnel had one unique feature—although only one line of rails entered the west portal, two emerged from the other end! The reason for this baffling phenomenon was simple (but still highly unusual). The passing loop at Haverthwaite began inside the tunnel, and, although this obviously helped the railway builders overcome the problem of lack of space, it created problems for the preservationists when they moved onto the line in 1970.

**The Preserved Section: Haverthwaite Station**

As was mentioned in chapter one, the building of Haverthwaite station was beset with difficulties as a result of the lack of space. Large quantities of solid rock had to be blasted away, both in the tunnels and in the intervening cutting, and the gangs of Irish navvies employed on the line lived in a shanty town situated in what is now the station yard. It is said that the huts—which had turf roofs—sprouted mushrooms after a spell of wet weather, and so provided the workers with an addition to their diet of beef and beer! The muscular railway builders were noted for their alcoholic capacity, and on Saturday nights they would retire to the local inns for mammoth drinking bouts. At the end of these sessions they would all contribute towards the cost of a barrel of beer, which would be rolled down the road to the station site ready for consumption on the following Sunday!

The completed station was provided with up and down platforms, with the main station buildings on the up side. Entry to the goods yard is by means of a long headshunt, which leaves the loop at its eastern end and then runs parallel to the main running line for about ¼-mile. The goods shed is situated behind the station buildings and is a standard Furness design, four bays long and built of "white brick" with red trimmings. To the south of the goods shed, the 3 ft. 6 in. gauge Low Wood Tramway once entered the yard from across the main road, and a small "white brick" hut was provided for the crossing keeper (this has recently been demolished in connection with the A590 road improvements).

The station served not only the village of Haverthwaite, but also the associated industrial hamlets of Low Wood and Backbarrow, and these little settlements generated a large amount of freight traffic. The sulphur and saltpetre needed in the gunpowder works were taken down to the bottom of the valley on the narrow-gauge tramway, while the finished product was transshipped in the same way. The Backbarrow iron works was also served by a direct rail connection, and the ore and limestone used in the furnaces arrived in mineral wagons which were taken down to the end of the headshunt—from where a loop and siding ran into the works. When, in about 1920, the Backbarrow furnaces changed from charcoal to coke fuel, the railway found itself with yet another major source of inward traffic. The pig iron produced at the plant left by rail, as did the dye produced in the old cotton mill.

Haverthwaite was the only passing place between Greenodd and Lakeside, and on occasions trains could be delayed for several minutes while waiting for workings from the opposite direction; for this reason, a local wit once suggested to Aslett that the station name be changed to "Have-a-wait"—he was not amused!

**The Preserved Section: Haverthwaite—Lakeside**

Accelerating away from Haverthwaite station on a 1 in 60 gradient, Lakeside-bound trains enter the 87-yard-long east tunnel and, still climbing, emerge onto a narrow shelf cut into the side of the valley. The headshunt, visible out of the right-hand windows, gives the impression that the trains are running on a double line, but after a short distance the second line of

**Above: Six months after the branch had been closed to all traffic, 5MT 4-6-0 No. 45134 pauses at Haverthwaite on September 2nd, 1967, with an enthusiasts' special. This was the last B.R. train to run up to Lakeside. (David Joy.) Below: A transformed scene at Haverthwaite, now the headquarters of the Lakeside Railway Society. "Cumbria" is leaving on a train while "Caliban" is prepared for later duty. (L.R.S.)**

**Above: 2-6-4T No. 2085 leaving Newby Bridge Halt with the 12-35 p.m. Haverthwaite-Lakeside. Opposite:— Top: 0-6-0ST "Princess" (front) and 0-4-0ST "Caliban". Bottom: L. & H.R. No. 5, an 0-6-0ST built by Hudswell Clarke in 1929. (Lakeside Railway Society.)**

65

**The steamer "Swift", launched in 1900, alongside the pavilion restaurant at Lakeside. The characteristic station buildings are on the right. (Sankey Collection.)**

**The original "Swan", the first of the Furness Railway steamers on Windermere, was launched on June 5th, 1869, and remained in service until 1938. She is seen here leaving Lakeside. (Sankey Collection.)**

rails stop just short of the abandoned Backbarrow works. These were one of the oldest continuously worked ironmaking sites in Britain; a bloomery forge was in existence by 1685, and a blast-furnace was in operation by 1711. The works—which are far smaller than one might have expected—are situated on a lower level than the railway, and this enabled ore to be gravity discharged from the sidings into the furnaces. It is interesting to recall that "Iron Mad" Wilkinson, the pioneering ironmaster, lived at Backbarrow as a young man and learnt part of his trade at the historic Backbarrow furnace. (His house can still be seen, some 200 yards south-east of the works.)

Passing the ironworks, and slowly turning onto a more northerly course, the railway continues along its narrow ledge with thickly-wooded coppices and plantations to the left and the turbulent waters of the Leven bubbling and cascading down below. The little hamlet of Backbarrow can be seen away on the far side of the valley, its dark grey slate houses clinging to the fellsides and giving the whole settlement more than a passing resemblance to a Welsh mining village. The hamlet looks pleasant enough now, but it is likely that at the height of the Industrial Revolution this remote mountain community endured much suffering and oppression. The settlement grew up to house the labour force which toiled in the nearby cotton mills, and several families would have shared each tenement. The now-demolished "apprentice house" was little better than a prison for the scores of pauper children who were recruited in workhouses as far away as London—records show that many of these children never grew to become adults; poor diet, long hours and unguarded machinery took a cruel toll. The mill itself closed in the 1860s, but the premises were later converted into an ultramarine (dolly blue) works and have continued as such up to the present day. The trains pass the mill some ¾-mile beyond the ironworks, and passengers who look back towards Haverthwaite will see a tremendous panorama, taking in the entire valley, with the cotton workers' houses, the ironworks and the many-windowed mill all clustered around the sparkling river Leven. Yet the scene—which is a typical 18th century industrial landscape—is in no way an ugly one; it is, as the landscape historian W. G. Hoskins has pointed out, "a busy landscape, full of detail and movement, like one of Brueghel's paintings".

Beyond Backbarrow the valley opens out and the gradient eases to 1 in 117. Still curving towards the north, the trains pass an inevitable Nonconformist chapel and then some workers' cottages which back right on to the line. A stone-built bridge carries a farm track across the railway before it turns to the north-east once more and crosses a minor road. The landscape is now heavily wooded, with dense foliage on both sides of the

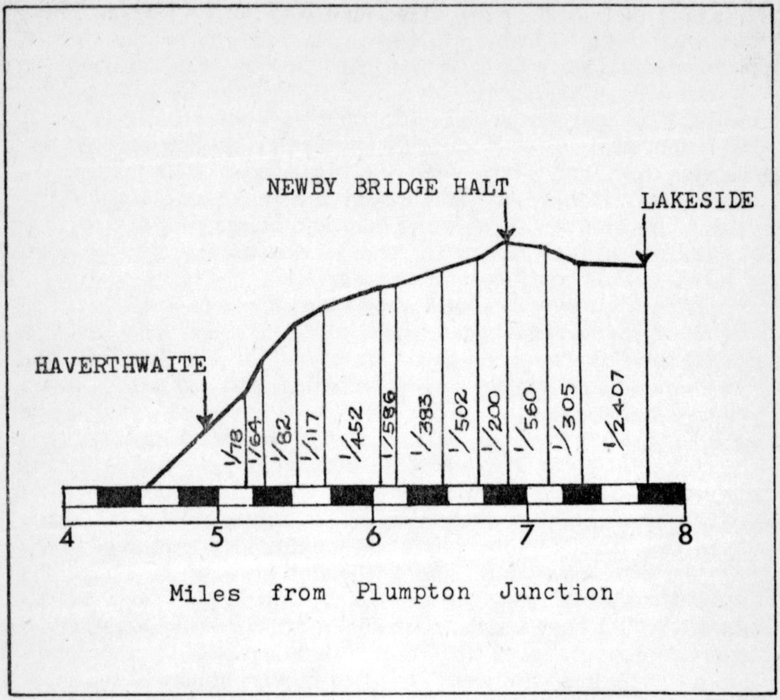


line, and the trains run dead straight for the next mile towards the impressive bulk of Gummer's How rising to over 1,000 ft. in the distance.

Passing a small Lakeland farmstead on the left-hand side of the line, the trains enter a short rock cutting before coming to rest in the platform at Newby Bridge, the only "Halt" on the Furness system. Newby Bridge, some seven miles from Plumpton Junction, marks the summit level of the line. Although, as we have seen, it was to have been a terminus, it consists of nothing but a short curving platform sandwiched between the river and the steeply-rising Finsthwaite Fells. A minor road, which crosses the railway at the southern end of the platform, curves round to run below the halt and then leads to the 18th century Swan Hotel—a large rambling coaching inn which stands next to the actual Newby Bridge. The bridge belongs to the 17th century, but it is likely that it utilises parts of earlier structures; the presence of some old stepping stones, just upstream of the bridge, underlines the antiquity of this site—the highest crossing place on the Leven.

Descending slightly beyond the halt, the line runs through another cutting and passes beneath the Newby Bridge to Lakeside road before levelling out for the final run into the Lakeside terminus. To the left, a row of gaunt-looking cottages comes into view; their "patent white bricks" (which in fact soon weathered to a creamish-yellow) suggest, quite rightly, that they were once railway houses. It is a matter of conjecture why the Furness should have chosen to build its employees' dwellings here rather than at the terminus unless, of course, they were built before the company had decided to extend the railway on to Lakeside.

Out of the right-hand windows of Lakeside-bound trains, travellers will see the back of the Swan Hotel with a wide reach of the Leven visible behind it. This was the site of the early terminus of the pre-railway steamers, and, looking at the shallow waters, one wonders how even a small boat could have managed to force its way up to the hotel. Indeed, the river was sometimes almost dry during the summer months—a situation that has recently been rectified by the construction of a new weir. The railway then curves to the left, and is almost immediately joined by the abandoned trackbed of a long siding which runs parallel to the main line on the landward side; this siding was entered from Lakeside station—still about ¾-mile away—and was used to stable excursion stock. In the line's Edwardian heyday, train after train could have been seen parked nose to tail all the way from the station to the buffers!

**Lakeside Terminus**

The final approach to Lakeside is highly scenic. With the waters of the lake virtually lapping the wheels of the trains, the track runs along a tree-lined "avenue" with Gummer's How forming a spectacular backdrop. A small cutting, spanned by the picturesque Landing How iron bridge, marks the end of the journey, and as the train slows for the final crawl to the buffers travellers can see the steamer slipway on the right-hand side of the line—in the old days it was common practice for locomotives to haul the ships up the slipway for their winter overhauls!

Lakeside (Windermere) station, situated some 3¼ miles from Haverthwaite, still looks like a main-line station, although the principal terminal buildings were pulled down when the steamer pier was consolidated by pile-driving to stop it sinking. The train shed, however, survives, and the actual lake-side buildings —which are now given over entirely to B.R's "Sea Link" Division —are still more extensive than one usually finds on preserved lines. The main structure is ten bays long, and the glass-fronted upper part is now known as the "Norseman" Restaurant; the Palm Court orchestra no longer plays, but it is still possible to sit in the restaurant and watch the comings and goings below on the landing stage.

The track layout at Lakeside is now reduced to a simple run-round loop with a spur at the end of the line, in order that both platforms can be used. The crossover beneath the overall roof is released from the signal box, which stands on the platform at the other end of the station. There were at one time six parallel sidings in Lakeside goods yard; one of these ended in the goods shed, and another ran into a single-road engine shed. The longest siding—on the landward side of the yard—continued across what is now the car park and ended on a wagon turntable. A second line of rails left the siding at 90 degrees and ran into a rather ugly coal dump situated right in front of the main station buildings. This unusual arrangement enabled coal for the steamers to be shovelled into narrow-gauge tramway wagons—which were then pushed by hand down onto the landing stage. The coal finally reached the ships' bunkers in locally-made baskets known as "swills". This method of fuelling ceased, of course, when the fleet was motorised, and all traces of the siding and tramway have disappeared.

At Lakeside our journey over the L. & H.R. must come to an end; the story, however, is not yet finished. The railway steamers on Winderemere are an important aspect of the line's existence, and we therefore continue our narrative with a short history of the railway fleet.

# 6. The Steamers on Windermere

THE first Windermere steamer was the *Lady of the Lake*, a wooden paddler built locally by Richard Ashburner of Greenodd for the pioneer Windermere Steam Yacht Company. When she was launched at Newby Bridge in 1845 she was the first steamer to operate on an English lake. She could carry about 200 passengers and was elaborately finished with a graceful clipper bow and a luxurious saloon, complete with carpets and mirrors. It is recorded that the band of the Kendal Cavalry entertained the guests on her maiden voyage! Ashburner—who built several small sailing vessels in his Greenodd yard before moving to Barrow in 1850—designed the *Lady of the Lake* as a screw steamer, but it was found that the water at Newby Bridge was too shallow for this plan to be carried out and paddles were fitted instead. The *Lady of the Lake* proved so successful that another ship, the *Lord of the Isles*, followed her into service in 1846. This second steamer was another wooden paddler, built by Ashburner and launched at Newby Bridge. Her life, unfortunately, was short, as she was destroyed by fire whilst moored to Bowness Pier in November 1850.

The rival Windermere Iron Steamboat Company, formed in 1849, owned two paddle steamers, the *Firefly* and the *Dragonfly*, both built by McConochie & Claud of Liverpool and assembled at Low Wood, near Ambleside, in 1849 and 1850 respectively. The appearance of these two new steamers sparked off a vicious war between the two operators. Rates were slashed and hand-bills and posters bombarded the public with rival propaganda claims; when some spares for the *Lady of the Lake* mysteriously disappeared, sabotage was widely suspected. Eventually, however, the two companies saw the advantages of amalgamation, and the Windermere United Steam Yacht Company was formed in 1858. The new concern ordered a further paddle steamer in 1866; the new vessel, the *Rothay*, was built by the Lancaster Ship Building Company and was the last steamer to be assembled and launched at Newby Bridge, as well as being the last paddle-steamer to enter service on the lake. The *Rothay* was 105 ft. long and had a rudder fore and aft—a boon in the cramped conditions at Newby Bridge.

The Furness Railway had meanwhile cast covetous eyes upon the steamer business, and the next steamer, the *Swan,* was built at the brand new slipway at Lakeside by T. B. Seath & Co. of Rutherglen, Glasgow. The *Swan* was considerably bigger than the earlier steamers, and was the first screw-driven vessel to enter the fleet. She measured 150 ft. in length with a beam of 18 ft. The launching of the *Swan,* at about 3 p.m. in the afternoon of Saturday, June 5th, 1869, was a truly grand occasion; about 2,000 people assembled at Lakeside to watch James Ramsden's wife, the Lady Mayoress of Barrow, perform the traditional ceremony. "On the signal being given", recorded the "Barrow Herald", "a few blows from the hammers of the workmen displaced the stays, and a flutter of excitement ran through the crowd. She stirred not, however, and almost breathless silence prevailed for a few moments whilst a little pressure was brought to bear upon the bows, upon which she began, almost imperceptibly at first, but every instant gathering increased momentum, to glide towards the water amidst the hearty cheers of all present, the firing of artillery and the strains of 'Rule Britannia' from the band. Just as she began to move, the Mayoress broke the bottle on her bow, and the bubbling wine showed that part of the ceremony to have been efficiently performed, and the *Swan* to have been duly christened."

The new steamer had a shallow hull, with well-decks fore and aft and a central saloon. A tall narrow smoke-stack projected through the roof of the saloon, and her canoe-shaped bows were graced by the figure of a swan. The 442 passengers could sit in the comfort of the saloon and watch the scenery glide past through the large plate glass windows, or move for'ard to the open bow section. Steps led up to the roof of the saloon, which formed a promenade deck with handrails and wooden seats. The steersman stood immediately for'ard of the smoke-stack in an open wheel-house, thereby gaining a good view from his rather exposed location. The *Swan,* together with the *Firefly, Dragonfly* and *Rothay,* was taken into direct railway ownership in 1872, and these four steamers handled the Windermere passenger services—which now operated from Lakeside instead of Newby Bridge—until 1879, when two new screw-steamers appeared. (The *Lady of the Lake* seems to have disappeared by the early 1870s.)

The waters of the lake were by this time quite crowded, with numerous pleasure craft of all shapes and sizes gliding to and fro. Small skiffs and sailing boats were the commonest types of vessel in this period, but mention must be made of one other form of pleasure boat—the steam yacht. Several were in operation on the lake—a reflection of the large numbers of rich Victorian businessmen who lived in the Windermere area. One of these great capitalists, the famous H. W. Schneider, one of the most powerful men in the local mining industry and among the original promoters of the Furness Railway, bought Belsfield House near Bowness and used his steam yacht, the *Esperance*, to take him down the lake to Lakeside station in the mornings and bring him back in the evenings. It is said that he would walk down to his private landing stage, preceded at a discreet distance by his butler, who carried a covered and heated silver tureen containing a lavish breakfast to be eaten on the six mile voyage to Lakeside. At the station, Schneider would climb aboard the Barrow train which would take him to his office for the day's business. The *Esperance*—which was later immortalised as Captain Flint's houseboat in Arthur Ransome's book "Swallows and Amazons"—was similar in appearance to the railway steamers and had a graceful clipper bow. It has been now privately restored and can still be seen steaming about on the lake.

In 1871 the Furness Railway introduced a bulky, bluff-bowed, barge-like steamer called the *Raven*, which carried freight traffic to and from the railhead at Lakeside and thereby gave the numerous scattered houses and settlements in the Windermere area a door-to-door goods service. The *Raven* was powered by a vertical boiler and steered by a long "rib-tickler" tiller. Two more passenger steamers, the *Teal* and the *Cygnet*, appeared in 1879. These two vessels, the first wholly railway-owned passenger steamers to join the fleet, were built by the Barrow Shipbuilding Company and assembled at Lakeside, the component parts coming to the slipway by train. The design of these near-identical screw steamers was similar to that of *Swan;* they had shallow hulls with raised central portions containing the engines, comfortable passenger saloons, and a tall, slender funnel projecting through the upper decks. Both vessels were 106 ft. long and were registered to carry 336 passengers. Their G.R.T. was 50 tons.

The next new steamer—the *Tern*—was launched at Lakeside in 1891. She was built by an Essex boatbuilding firm, Forrest & Son of Wivenhoe, and was very similar to the *Teal* and *Cygnet*. The *Tern* was, however, somewhat bigger, with a length of 146 ft., an 18 ft beam, and a G.R.T. of 120 tons. Her saloon was also larger than those of the earlier vessels, so that, although she was not quite as long as the 150 ft. *Swan*, she could carry considerably more passengers (633 to the *Swan's* 442). The new steamer's external appearance was enhanced by unusual "canoe"-shaped bows and a finely formed counter stern.

The increasing number of Lake District tourists meant that yet another steamer was needed, and in 1900 the 203-ton *Swift* glided down the slipway at Lakeside. Built, like the *Swan*, by Seath of Rutherglen, this twin screw steamer was 158 ft. long with a 21 ft. beam. She was powered by a four-cylinder compound engine and had a locomotive-type boiler; her cruising speed was 12 knots and she could accommodate 781 passengers. She was, arguably, the finest steamer ever to sail on the lake; built in an age which produced such oceanic greyhounds as the *Mauretania* and the *Aquitania*, the *Swift* had the lines of a true thoroughbred with a distinct sheer running from her straight stem to her delicate, cut-away stern. A tall, raked funnel suggested power, and, combined with her moulded lines, gave her a safe, "seaworthy" appearance. One feels that she could have battled her way through a turbulent ocean were she not confined to the (relatively) tranquil waters of a lake. Not only did the *Swift* look powerful and seaworthy, she also marked a considerable advance in design in that she was fully decked with extensive passenger accommodation "down below". Large square ports allowed the passengers to view the scenery from the saloons, or they could sit up on deck (and brave the elements!).

There was now an extensive railway-owned fleet in operation on the lake. Nevertheless, when in 1907 the luxury steam yacht *Britannia* came on the market, she was snapped up at the bargain price of £360. This vessel, which was again a product of Seath's yards, had been originally built in 1879 for a private customer. She had cost £12,000—a fantastic sum when one considers that the stately *Swift* had cost only £9,500—and had the hull of a clipper, complete with cut-away stem and a long bowsprit. She was 110 ft. long and had raked masts and funnel; she was, in fact, quite an impressive vessel, being equal in size to the older steamers but not as big as the *Tern* or *Swift*. Her main duty, however, was as a private charter vessel, and she was not used in regular timetable service.

The post-First World War period saw few changes on the lake. The *Britannia*—an obsolete relic of a less egalitarian age—was sold for scrapping in 1919, but the *Swan, Cygnet, Teal, Tern* and *Swift* continued to sail up and down the lake throughout the 1920s and 1930s; these are, in fact, the steamers which feature in Arthur Ransome's famous children's books. In those days they were of course **real** steamers; most of the Windermere vessels were equipped with simple non-condensing engines, which meant that their exhaust was "puffed" out like that of a locomotive. Yet those who knew and travelled on them maintain that the exhaust was not in the least troublesome, and argue that the tremor-free progress and gentle rhythm of the steam-driven craft was far preferable to the noise and vibration experienced aboard the present-day diesel-powered fleet. However, steam slowly gave way to the internal-combustion engine, starting in 1924 when the *Cygnet* was converted to a motor vessel for reasons of economy.

In 1936 the "diesel invasion" began in earnest when the L.M.S.

launched the motor vessel *Teal* from the slipway at Lakeside. This second *Teal* was built by Vickers-Armstrong of Barrow, and brought up to the lake in sections on special trains. The design of the vessel broke new ground in that, for the first time, three decks were provided—a lower saloon within the hull, an upper saloon on the main deck, and an open upper deck. A bridge was built onto the for'ard end of the upper deck, thereby creating a fourth tier—critics, comparing the new vessel to the older steamers, likened her to a "floating wedding cake!". *Teal II* can carry over 800 holidaymakers, and she has a Gross Registered Tonnage of 251 tons. A sister ship, the M.V. *Swan,* was launched at Lakeside two years later, and the appearance of these two large motor vessels heralded the demise of the old *Teal* and the earlier *Swan;* they were withdrawn in 1936 and 1938 respectively, and both were scrapped. A happier fate befell the *Cygnet*—she passed into private ownership and is still occasionally seen on the lake. By 1938 the composition of the railway fleet on Windermere had reached its final form, and the vessels in service included the S.S. *Swift,* the S.S. *Tern,* the M.V. *Teal II* and the M.V. *Swan II.* The S.S. *Raven,* too, could often be seen at Lakeside, although she was no longer railway-owned; in 1927 the L.M.S. sold her to Vickers-Armstrong, and her new owners used her for armament experiments carried out on the lake.

The most momentous change to take place in post-war years has been the complete change-over from steam to diesel propulsion. Both the *Swift* and the *Tern* are now motor vessels, and both have had their tall Victorian funnels replaced by squat, streamlined affairs. In the case of the *Tern* this did perhaps bring about an improvement in appearance. Her original funnel was far too slender, and looked rather like a stove-pipe; the much fatter chimney carried today makes her look more normal. The *Swift,* on the other hand, looked better with her original smokestack, and her new funnel sits strangely on her straight-stemmed Victorian hull. Nevertheless, the *Swift* is still the most impressive member of the fleet; bigger than the *Tern,* she does not suffer from the "unfinished" appearance of the *Swan* and the *Teal*—although, if these two vessels ever sprouted chimneys, their looks would be immeasurably improved.

**A Voyage on the Lake**

A journey on the Windermere steamers is essentially a quiet, leisurely affair; one can book tickets at Haverthwaite, Lakeside, Bowness or Ambleside, and the round trip—a journey of 20 miles or so—takes from two to three hours (depending on the point of embarkation). Lakeside, the home "port" of the fleet, has changed little over the years, and the ships are still re-fitted here every

## SUMMARY OF STEAMERS MENTIONED IN TEXT

| NAME | TYPE | BUILDERS | DATE | NOTES |
|---|---|---|---|---|
| Lady of the Lake | Paddle steamer | Ashburner of of Greenodd | 1845 | scrapped |
| Lord of the Isles | Paddle steamer | Ashburner of of Greenodd | 1846 | destroyed by fire, 1850 |
| Firefly | Paddle steamer | McConochie & Claud, Liverpool | 1849 | scrapped |
| Dragonfly | Paddle steamer | McConochie & Claud, Liverpool | 1850 | scrapped |
| Rothay | Paddle steamer | Lancaster Shipbuilding Co. | 1866 | scrapped |
| Swan | Twin screw steamer | Seath of Rutherglen | 1869 | scrapped 1938 |
| Raven | Single screw steamer | Seath of Rutherglen | 1871 | sold 1927 |
| Cygnet | Twin screw steamer | Barrow Shipbuilding Co. | 1879 | converted to private yacht |
| Teal | Twin screw steamer | Barrow Shipbuilding Co. | 1879 | scrapped 1936 |
| Britannia | Twin screw steamer | Seath of Rutherglen | 1879 | scrapped 1919 |
| Tern | Twin screw steamer | Forrest of Wivenhoe | 1891 | Passed into B.R. ownership |
| Swift | Twin screw steamer | Seath of Rutherglen | 1900 | Passed into B.R. ownership |
| Teal II | Twin screw motor vessel | Vickers Armstrong | 1936 | Passed into B.R. ownership |
| Swan II | Twin screw motor vessel | Vickers Armstrong | 1938 | Passed into B.R. ownership |

winter, the ships' crews doing the necessary work.

The lower reaches of the lake are tamer than the upper, but the wooded slopes visible on either side, together with the more distant fells, combine to produce an exceedingly picturesque effect. The Storrs Hall Hotel—some 5 miles from Lakeside—marks the site of a former landing place, but Bowness Pier, $1\frac{3}{4}$ miles beyond, is now the first port of call. The short pier, with its ornate Victorian booking office and enamel B.R. signs, looks rather like a railway station without its tracks—and indeed the "Railway Clearing House Gazetteer" classifies both Bowness and Ambleside piers as passenger-only stations. Readers of "Swallows and Amazons" will note that Bowness is Arthur Ransome's "Rio Bay". The "steamers" come alongside Bowness Pier with their bows pointing towards the shore, and the departure for Ambleside is marked by much threshing of water as the twin-screwed vessels leave the pier stern-first, and then swing their bows northwards for the final stage of the voyage.

The northern end of the lake is usually less congested than the Lakeside end, and, with fewer dinghys and skiffs to get in the way, the "steamers" can steer a straight course towards the dark, sombre peaks beyond Ambleside. The atmosphere seems to change as the "steamers" near Ambleside; the lake is broader here, the wind seems to blow malignantly, and the surrounding mountains impart a gloomy aspect to the scene—especially on a dull day. One becomes conscious of the fact that water is not man's natural element, and remembers tales of storms and tempests long ago. The lake can in fact be a dangerous place, and on occasions freak storms have whipped it up into a mini-ocean complete with big, white-topped waves. It was during one such storm that the first *Swan*—tied too securely to the jetty at Lakeside—was swamped by the rising surface of the lake and sent to the bottom (little damage was sustained, however, and she was raised with the aid of pontoons).

Ambleside Pier—the northern terminus of the "steamer" service—is actually at Waterhead; Ambleside itself is situated $\frac{3}{4}$-mile away to the north. The pier, with its wooden booking office, is similar to that at Bowness, but, apart from the large Youth Hostel, some hotels and a few houses, there is little else at Waterhead. Ten minutes "turn round" time is allowed at Ambleside, and then the ships return to Bowness and the crowded southern reaches of the lake. In all, the voyage from Lakeside to Ambleside is a fascinating experience, and anyone contemplating a journey on the L. & H.R. would be well advised to allow time for a further trip on the *Tern, Swift, Teal* or *Swan.* (Alternatively, one can travel to the L. & H.R. via Oxenholme and Windermere, taking advantage of the bus connections between Windermere station and Bowness Pier, which link the steamers to the rest of the B.R. network.)

## A Note on the other Furness Steamers

The F.R. owned two further steamers on Coniston Lake. The *Gondola* was a very small vessel looking rather like a canal packet boat. The *Lady of the Lake,* on the other hand (not to be confused with the pioneer Windermere steamer), was a larger vessel, generally similar to the *Tern,* with canoe-shaped bows and a bell-mouthed funnel.

The first steamer used on the Fleetwood—Barrow service was the P.S. *Lady Evelyn.* She was purchased new in 1900, and could carry 714 passengers. A second ship, the P.S. *Lady Margaret,* was purchased from P. & R. Campbell Ltd. in 1903, but she was sold to the Admiralty in 1908 and replaced by the P.S. *Philomel.* A fourth ship, the P.S. *Lady Moyra,* was purchased in 1910; she achieved fame as a result of her record passage from Barrow to Fleetwood in a time of 45 minutes—about half an hour faster than usual. The *Philomel* was little used after the arrival of the *Lady Moyra* and was sold in 1913. The two surviving steamers—the *Lady Evelyn* and *Lady Moyra*—were requisitioned by the Admiralty during the First World War, and both were sold in 1918; the Fleetwood service was never re-instated.

The Windermere and Coniston steamers emerged from the Great War as the Furness Railway's only passenger-carrying vessels. It is interesting to recall, however, that the *Swift* and *Tern's* two ocean-going sisters sailed on throughout the 1920s and 1930s as the Bristol Channel steamers *Brighton Belle* and *Brighton Queen.* They were requisitioned again in 1939 and, equipped with guns and search lights and painted battleship grey, they saw service as anti-aircraft ships. Finally, in May 1940 they were sent across the English Channel to assist with the Dunkirk rescue operations, and there, amid the fire and smoke of battle, their long careers came to an end.

# 7. The Gunpowder Tramways

THE gunpowder works at Low Wood and Black Beck have already been mentioned in connection with the traffic carried on the railway. It was felt, however, that, in view of the interesting tramways which linked the two works to the Lakeside branch, it would be worth devoting the final chapter to the subject. The Lakeland gunpowder industry grew up to serve the local mining and quarrying industries. The Furness district, with its sparsely-inhabited countryside and fast-flowing streams (to drive the mills), was particularly suitable for the industry. Furthermore, the well-wooded slopes of the Leven and Rusland Pool valleys afforded natural protection and at the same time yielded charcoal—one of the three ingredients of gunpowder. Before the coming of the railway, the other two ingredients—sulphur and saltpetre—were brought to the mills via the port of Greenodd and then taken up the Leven and Rusland Pool in barges. The opening of the Lakeside branch in 1869 changed all this, and both works were soon making use of the new form of transport. As we have seen, Black Beck works (opened in 1862) was connected to the main line by a two-mile long private branch line, while the Low Wood works (1799) made use of a narrow-gauge system.

The Black Beck branch, known as "Dixon's Siding" after the original owner of the works, left the main line near Lady Syke bridge and ran up the valley of the Rusland Pool to the works, which were situated near the hamlet of Bouth. The only engineering work of any note was a timber trestle viaduct across the Rusland Pool. On reaching the works, the line branched out to serve the various small mills used to prepare and mix the powder (for obvious reasons these were widely dispersed and were protected by banks and screens of trees). Horse haulage was used throughout, both on the "main line" and within the works itself, and the two sidings at the junction formed a small "exchange yard". The actual junction was controlled by a ground frame, the key to which was obtained from either Haverthwaite or Greenodd boxes. The tramway was dismantled following the closure of the Black Beck works in 1928, but its route can quite easily be traced, earthworks being visible for most of its length. Part of the route has been converted into a roadway to serve the caravan park which now stands on the site of the works.

The Low Wood tramway was of 3 ft. 6 in. gauge, and ran from Haverthwaite station yard across the A590 road and down the side of the valley to the works. The road crossing was unprotected by gates, and when, in the latter years of the tramway, motor traffic started to increase, it was usual for L.M.S. men to go out onto the road to halt the cars when the crossing was in use. A reversal was necessary shortly after the tramway crossed the road, and after a short distance travelling in the opposite direction, losing height all the time, the line entered a second reversing point. It then dropped steeply in a great curve down to the river. The Leven was crossed by a girder bridge at a point where the waters were channelled through a deep narrow gorge; it is possible that this bridge—which is still in existence—is a relatively modern replacement of an original trestle bridge. On reaching the east bank of the Leven, the tramway spread out among the various mills which, like those at Black Beck, were widely dispersed to minimise the effects of explosions. A "main line" ran through the complex and crossed the B5278 on the level, and continued in a south-westerly direction as a roadside tramway until it reached the company's powder magazine in Roudsea Wood. One of the iron crossing-gates can still be seen at the B5278 crossing.

As at Black Beck, the motive power for the Low Wood tramway was the horse, since no locomotives were allowed in the works. The animals used were shod with copper shoes, and it is possible that the rails on the site were also of non-ferrous metal. The only "steam engine" on the site is still there—a stationary boiler, manufactured by J. Robey & Son, stands intact, though rusty, in the drying house.

Rolling stock consisted of plank wagons and covered vans, some of which are, incredibly, still in existence at Low Wood. In keeping with usual narrow-gauge practice, they had centre buffer/couplings. More unusual was the provision of brakesmen's seats on the ends of the vehicles to enable them to be gravity worked down to the factory (the horses returned through the wood and across the bridge on their own). On the descent the brakesmen checked the progress of their vehicles by applying pressure on the brake handles, but within the works themselves it appears that some of the men preferred to control the wagons by keeping their thick-soled boots in contact with the inside edges of the rails! The surviving rolling stock is maroon in colour—probably as originally painted. The two surviving plank wagons are in a very decrepit state, having stood out in the open, surrounded by damp undergrowth since the 1930s. The four box vans, however, have fared better, and one is in excellent condition, having stood for many years, complete with its wheels, on a concrete base. Of the track itself, little remains, although the sleepers of the "main line" are still in situ for 200-300 yards. The rails were lifted a few years after closure of the works in 1935, possibly as scrap metal for the war effort; as late as 1948, however, the level crossing over the B5278 was still in existence complete with rails.

Accidents and explosions took place quite frequently in the early years, which is hardly surprising when one considers some of the things that went on; it was not uncommon, for instance, for cartridges to be filled by candlelight! By the time the railway had reached Low Wood, safety precautions had tightened up; nevertheless, explosions still occurred, and there were several "near misses" on the Haverthwaite road crossing. The one spectacular accident of recent times took place on the main line and involved a Lancashire & Yorkshire 2-4-2T which, on July 15th, 1932, was shunting at Backbarrow Ironworks. It was usual to shunt the in-coming wagons—loaded with ore and coke—up the gradient to the buffers at the end of the headshunt. The engine would then uncouple and go into the ironworks to bring out the loaded pig iron wagons, which were then coupled up to those carrying ore and coke in order that the latter could be shunted into the works. On the day in question, however, the combined weight of all the ore, coke and pig-iron wagons proved too much for the 2-4-2T, which was, after all, a passenger engine, and the 55 ton locomotive was slowly pushed back down the headshunt towards Haverthwaite station. The crew "abandoned ship" as the cavalcade slipped out of the tunnel and onto the outer siding in the goods yard; horrified, they watched their engine slither towards an L.N.E.R. box van and an L.M.S. gunpowder van, which stood at the end of the siding. The impact pushed the two vans through the buffers and into the road. Fortunately, there was no explosion (possibly the gunpowder van was empty!), but the engine ended up with its front axle buried in the ground and was not re-railed until 03-30 the following morning.

Such, briefly, is the history of the Black Beck and Low Wood gunpowder tramways; those interested in a more detailed account of the industry should consult the work of Dr. J. D. Marshall and Mr. M. Davies-Shiel (see bibliography). Finally, it must be pointed out that, although the tramways themselves can be seen from public rights of way, the sites of the two works themselves are private property.

# Sources and Bibliography

This work does not claim to be an example of great scholarship. Nevertheless, the following primary sources were used to piece together the early history of the branch: "The Barrow Herald", "Bradshaw's Shareholders' Guides" and "The Railway Times". A bibliography of secondary sources is given below. There has in fact been very little of note written on the Furness Railway; the only serious study is *Furness & the Industrial Revolution.* Rush largely repeats Marshall, but nevertheless contains useful details of F.R. rolling stock. The best short history, however, will be found in Joy. W. Hardin Osborne's articles were invaluable for details of the Edwardian era, while Duckworth & Langmuir provide details of other F.R. steamers, together with further pictures of the Coniston and Windermere steamers.


Duckworth & Langmuir, *Railway & Other Steamers.*

Alan Harris, "Seaside Resorts of the North West", *Transactions of the Historic Society of Lancashire & Cheshire,* Vol. 115, 1963.

S. C. Jenkins, "The Lakeside Branch", *Railway Modeller,* Vol. 27, July 1976.

Norman Jones, "Lakeland's Steamers", *The Meccano Magazine,* XLVI, 1961.

J. D. Marshall, *Furness & the Industrial Revolution,* 1958.

J. D. Marshall & M. Davies-Shiel, *The Industrial Archaeology of the Lake Counties,* 1969.

R. W. Rush, *The Furness Railway,* 1973.

R. W. Rush, *Furness Locomotives & Rolling Stock,* 1973.

David Joy, *Cumbrian Coast Railways,* 1968.

W. Hardin Osborne, "A Furness Miscellany", *Railway Modeller,* Vol. 13, 1962.

W. Hardin Osborne, "Lakeside (Windermere)", *loc. cit.,* Vol. 16, May 1965.

W. Hardin Osborne, "Steam Yacht Cygnet", *loc. cit.,* Vol. 16, Oct., 1965.

W. Hardin Osborne, "Lakeside Memories", *The Iron Horse,* Summer, 1969.

W. Hardin Osborne, "Furness Locomotives on the Lakeside Branch", *The Iron Horse,* Spring 1970.

W. Hardin Osborne, "The Furness Railway's Steamers on Windermere", *The Iron Horse,* Spring 1971.

H. I. Quayle, "Gunpowder Railways of Southern Lakeland", *The Railway World*, 1973.

H. I. Quayle, "The Low Wood Tramway", *The Iron Horse,* Summer 1971.